THE NATURE OF THE HUMAN SOUL

THE NATURE OF THE HUMAN SOUL

Philosophical Anthropology & Moral Theology

Sr. Mary Angelica Neenan, O.P.

With a Foreword by Wojciech Giertych, O.P.

CLUNY

Providence, Rhode Island

CLUNY MEDIA EDITION, 2017

The Nature of the Human Soul copyright © 2017
by The Dominican Sisters of St. Cecilia Congregation

Cluny Media edition copyright © 2017 by Cluny Media LLC

ISBN: 9781944418335

❧ VISIT CLUNY ONLINE AT WWW.CLUNYMEDIA.COM ❧

NIHIL OBSTAT:
Rev. John P. Cush, S.T.L., S.T.D. (Cand.),
Censor Deputatus

IMPRIMATUR:
Most Rev. David R. Choby, D.D., J.C.L.,
Bishop of Nashville

Cover design by Clarke & Clarke
Cover artwork: Masolino da Panicale, *Annunciation*,
c. 1423–1424 or c. 1427–1429, tempera on panel
Courtesy of Wikimedia Commons

TABLE OF CONTENTS

To all my students, past, present, and future.

May this book assist students of Moral Theology in understanding the gifts that God has given to each human soul by nature and by grace. May these students grow in truth, in love, and in freedom so as to live for the glory of God and come to fulfillment in perfect union with Him.

FOREWORD

There are some questions from which we cannot escape. We may ignore them, put them aside or forget about them, but ultimately they will hit us—or something else will hit us, if we fail to deal with these questions and fail to find the answers. We all want to be happy but we have difficulty in understanding what is happiness and what is it that can really make us happy. We all have an intellect and a will, but we also have emotions that sometimes engage us and make us do things that we did not really want to do, and yet we did them, and as a result we are unhappy, even though the emotions did furnish some passionate feelings, pleasant or perplexing. But happiness does not consist in just experiencing feelings. In fact, happiness consists in having more and more problems, always of a higher order. As we react to these problems, creatively, in truth and with love and responsibility, we experience happiness.

We are not the only people in the world who are raising such questions. Many have raised them before us and they have found answers that are true. Their accumulated wisdom allows us to understand ourselves and our actions better. It may also help us to sort ourselves out and to make sensible decisions about our lives. Just as there is the knowledge of the empirical sciences, worked out through observation, reflection and experimentation, which we can study, so there is a worked out and accumulated ethical knowledge about the human person, the soul, the spiritual faculties of the intellect and the will and the emotions that are conditioned by our bodies. A clear understanding of how all this works together is extremely useful, because even a minor error in the perception of our nature leads to serious errors in self-understanding, and what is more, in our lives. We all have only one life, and since time is in constant flux, we cannot go back and repeat some stages of our life, whenever we go wrong. We may repent and correct errors. We may plan the future better, but some consequences of our erroneous perceptions and rash decisions will be with us forever.

Happily, we do not have only our minds and our own experiences as sources of light. We can accede to the accumulated wisdom of previous generations of serious teachers who have thought about these issues, and have come to clear conclusions. A study of their teachings is of great use. But not only they can be our guides. In His goodness, God has given us His Word that was made manifest in His Son, Our Lord Jesus Christ. His utter gift of self, given on the Cross that turned out in its love to be more powerful than sin and death is the ultimate answer. Coupled with His teaching that we find in the Gospels, we have a divine source of orientation for our way. And what is strange is the fact that the answer has been given to us, even before we started asking the questions!

We need to put all this together, in our minds, our hearts, our decision-making, and our capacity for good, virtuous action. Only then the intellectual and moral tools that are necessary on the way of life will be at our disposal.

Now is the time to think about all this!

~Rev. Wojciech Giertych, O.P.
Rome, Italy
September, 2014

ACKNOWLEDGMENTS

The idea for this book originally began with the desire to copy my teaching notes for my students in order to provide something written to which they could refer while studying for my Moral Theology course. The course is at an introductory level, and often I need to cover the material in this book quickly. Every semester for the past nine or ten years, my students have requested more information about the nature of the soul, especially the nature of the intellect, will, and emotions, because they find it fascinating and want to know more. When I realized that I would be truncating some of this material while teaching in Italy for the study abroad program, I took the time to organize my teaching notes into this book. I owe my understanding of the thought of St. Thomas Aquinas to the kind help of Father Wojciech Giertych, O.P., who directed my dissertation, of which this little book is a small fruit. With the generosity and encouragement of our Architect, the book was translated into Italian and was first published in Rome.

This English-only edition is a result of the request of some Sisters in my community, without whose prayers, patience and hope this book would not have materialized.

~Sr. Mary Angelica Neenan, O.P.
St. Cecilia Motherhouse, Nashville, TN
Feast of St. Bonaventure, 2017

INTRODUCTION

When we study Moral Theology, we are trying to learn about God, especially as He works in our human actions, so as to be united with Him, truly happy. We do not just study the morality of human actions by themselves, but St. Thomas tries to show the fecundity (fruitfulness) of God in human actions, making the divine love of God real, apparent in human beings. It is not just looking at human actions with divine assistance, but seeing God's presence and action in real people and their actions. This can only be understood by faith, and possible by grace.

Morality is not about what is permitted or not permitted, what is against the rules, what is against the law (natural law, law of God, Canon Law, etc.), what are sins and penances, etc. Nor is it primarily centered on virtues and vices (virtue-based ethics), or centered on obligations (duty-based ethics). In the context of a Thomistic, indeed, a Christian, understanding of morality, morality is about what is the goal of man, what is the complete fulfilment of man's nature—that is union with God in eternal happiness. In order to pursue this study, we need to know something about what the true goal really is (who God really is, the nature of God, and the nature of the happiness He wants to give us), man's true capacities to achieve this goal (man's true nature, his faculties of body and soul), and how grace brings that nature to perfection.

Happiness is man's true call. This is what every man desires. Understanding that every man desires true happiness, we come to a series of questions regarding the nature of man. What is man? What is he capable of doing? What is true liberty? How does man achieve happiness? Where in his soul does happiness reside? These are the questions that lead us into a basic presentation of philosophical anthropology before discussing the nature of human action itself.

QUESTIONS

1. What is the purpose of studying morality? What major topics are included? Would you add any topics?

2. What topics are not the focus of morality? Why?

3. Why might students assume that the study of morality is limited to the topics in #2? How does this misconception come about?

4. What is "philosophical anthropology" and why is this a necessary foundation for any study of morality?

APPLICATION

Find the *Catechism of the Catholic Church*, either online or in hardcopy form, take a look at the table of contents and answer: Where is the section on the Life in Christ (morality) placed? What comes before it? What comes after it? Explain the possible logic behind this ordering.

CHAPTER ONE

Philosophical Anthropology

I. What is Man?

Man is a creature, a rational animal, a unique unity of body and spirit. Man is the apex of corporeal creation and at the same time, the lowest of spiritual creatures. He is a unique blend of the physical and spiritual world, having powers belonging to each as well as limitations belonging to each. As in all creatures, the soul animates the body. That means that the body cannot exist without its proper soul, which gives it life, gives it the capacity to perform its regular functions, and "encompasses"[1] the body. In fact, a separation of body and soul is the equivalent of death.

Every human soul is created directly by God.[2] Unique and unrepeatable, even when it comes to identical twins, each human soul is created for the purpose of a loving communion with God. Each human soul, in a unique and unrepeatable way, is capable of loving God and receiving His Divine Love. In order to see how this is possible, we need to understand the basic capacities of the human soul in general.

II. The Faculties of the Human Soul

1. The Vegetative Powers: Powers that seem to be only "of the body" are actually powers of the soul which animate the body. Although these powers require bodily functions, the animating principle is the soul.

- Nutrition.
- Growth.
- Reproduction.

(Photosynthesis is an example of a power of a plant soul, not found in a developed way in the human soul, because it is not needed.)

2. The Sensitive Powers: The sensitive powers allow the living being to interact with and respond to the outside world.

- Locomotion (self-movement).
- Five external senses—hearing, sight, smell, touch, and taste.
- Four internal senses—memory, imagination, common sense, and estimative sense.

---

1. Thomas Aquinas, *Summa Theologiae* (henceforth referred to as *ST*) I, q. 76, a. 3.

2. *Catechism of the Catholic Church* (Vatican City: Libreria Editrice Vaticana, 1997), §33: "The human person: with his openness to truth and beauty, his sense of moral goodness, his freedom and the voice of his conscience, with his longings for the infinite and for happiness, man questions himself about God's existence. In all this he discerns signs of his spiritual soul. The soul, the 'seed of eternity we bear in ourselves, irreducible to the merely material,' (*Gaudium et Spes*, §18) can have its origin only in God."

- Eleven emotions (passions).
  - Concupiscible appetite is attraction to pleasure (whether trying to obtain an easily obtainable good, or avoiding an easily avoidable evil).
  - Irascible appetite is responding to/desiring a difficult good or avoiding a difficult evil.

These appetites of the sensitive powers are aroused by stimuli (whether inside or outside of us).

3. The Intellective Powers:

A. The intellect. The intellect is the faculty of the soul for knowing (the truth). The rational faculty in man is combined with the will, although it has its own proper nature and operation. It is by the intellect that man can know universals and particulars, and can combine information in such a way as to reach conclusions. The nature of the intellect and its operations will be discussed in Chapter Three.

B. The will. Sometimes called the rational appetite, the will is the intellectual faculty of desire. The will is the faculty of the soul which desires the good, as such. The will always acts in conjunction with the intellect, for it is dependent on the intellect for perceiving a good, but the will has its own proper nature and operations which will be discussed in Chapter 3.

C. The interaction of the intellect and the will results in *freedom*.

In Chapter Two, we will consider more in depths the particular set of sensitive powers that have a strong bearing on our daily life, the emotions (or the passions). After that we will consider the two intellective powers, the intellect and will, the nature of each (Chapter Three), and finally the interaction of each which constitutes human freedom (Chapter Four). It is in this context of freedom that we can understand human actions and the working of grace. This is the reason for an examination of these faculties of the human soul—to better understand how man is made, and how God brings us gently and lovingly to our true happiness which is ultimately union with Him.

QUESTIONS

1. What is unique about the nature of the human person? How do we differ from other parts of creation?

2. In your own words, explain the relationship of the body and the soul. How does the classic Thomistic emphasis on the unity of man differ from the way most people imagine the body and soul to be related?

3. What is the human person created for and how can an understanding of the powers (capacities) of the human soul help to us to understand our purpose and dignity?

4. Create a list or a chart that helps you to identify and explain the faculties of the human soul. Indicate which faculties we share with animals and which faculties set us apart.

5. Why does the interaction of the intellect and will form the foundation of freedom?

6. St. Thomas Aquinas states that you cannot love what you do not know. Do you agree or disagree? Why or why not?

APPLICATION

What topics from the Introduction, questions #1 and #2, most interest you? How would a study of the faculties of the soul relate to and assist with your study of these questions?

APPLICATION

John Mayer sang, "I'm bigger than my body gives me credit for" (*Heavier Things*, 2003). Is there any truth to this statement? Are there any perils to this line of thought/lyricism?

Chapter Two

The Emotions

The emotions are "movements" of the sense appetite, whereby something is received (hence the classical term for them is *passions*). An emotion is a psychic reaction to any stimulus (either interior or exterior to the agent): either an attraction to something (perceived as good) or an aversion (something perceived as evil). Emotions respond in a corporeal and natural way, and have a physical effect. This *ability to be moved* is said to be a power.

Remember that the emotions can also be moved by the intellect and will, and in fact, the will relies on the intellect to interpret the emotion correctly. For example, a six-year-old child spills a glass of milk, and the mother goes into a screaming rage and spanks the child. One should assume that there is a deeper, underlying reason for the mother's over-reaction of anger (maybe she had a fight with her husband that morning and the anger stewed for hours until it came out this way). By not recognizing where her anger is really coming from, the emotion gets stronger and more out of control. Or suppose that there was no previous event, this outburst of anger is a result of her (warped) thinking—she had just been thinking how she never wanted this child in the first place, this child has cost her so much time and energy, she had to leave her job, change her life, she cannot do anything for herself anymore, she is not free to just go shopping, etc., and suddenly the child spills the milk.

This is a clear example of how our reasoning also directs our emotions. The emotions *do* in fact respond to our reasoning (which is our perception of reality), whether we like it or not! This fact shows us at once our dignity, and the extent of our fallenness. And we have yet another application of how the truth can set you free. The truth about reality will actually help our emotions to respond according to it.

We do not forget that the will is also a key player in guiding our emotions—the will can conjure up emotions (by commanding the memory to remember something, or to imagine something in order to get certain emotions). And also the will is needed to resist certain emotions (not voluntarily conjured). For example, when fear overtakes a person, her first inclination might be to run away, but by exercising her powers of intellect and will, she can talk to herself ("This is not something worthy of such fear," or "It is okay to feel afraid, but love conquers fear," etc.), and she can command herself to remain and endure or fight whatever it is.

Thus, St. Thomas Aquinas says that the emotions respond to the cogitative powers (reason and will), as well as the sensations of the body, imagination, memory, instinct, and estimative powers. The emotions can resist reason also, inasmuch as we sense or imagine something pleasant which reason forbids, or unpleasant which reason commands.[1] Just because they resist, however, does not mean that they cannot obey or cannot be guided.[2] This is not to deny that the sensitive appetites have their own proper power, but only to underline the interaction between the intellective powers and the sensitive powers in man, which will be described in the next chapter.

The emotions also respond to *each other* and *the environment*. The emotions respond to good and evil in different ways; and can be divided into categories according to how each emotion is moved, and in turn moves. Before dividing

---

1. For more by St. Thomas, see *ST* I, q. 81, a. 3, especially the reply to objection 2: "But the intellect or reason is said to rule the irascible and concupiscible by a politic power: because the sensitive appetite has something of its own, by virtue whereof it can resist the commands of reason. For the sensitive appetite is naturally moved, not only by the estimative power in other animals, and in man by the cogitative power which the universal reason guides, but also by the imagination and sense. Whence it is that we experience that the irascible and concupiscible powers do resist reason, inasmuch as we sense or imagine something pleasant, which reason forbids, or unpleasant, which reason commands. And so from the fact that the irascible and concupiscible resist reason in something, we must not conclude that they do not obey."

2. *ST* I-II, q. 17, a. 7: "Consequently in order to understand in what manner the act of the sensitive appetite is subject to the command of reason, we must consider in what manner it is in our power. Now it must be observed that the sensitive appetite differs from the intellective appetite, which is called the will, in the fact that the sensitive appetite is a power of a corporeal organ, whereas the will is not. Again, every act of a power that uses a corporeal organ, depends not only on a power of the soul, but also on the disposition of that corporeal organ: thus the act of vision depends on the power of sight, and on the condition of the eye, which condition is a help or a hindrance to that act. Consequently the act of the sensitive appetite depends not only on the appetitive power, but also on the disposition of the body. [CONT.]

the emotions into the categories of concupiscible and irascible, we can say some things of all emotions in general.

I. Emotions in General

1. All emotions are caused by love because love is the emotion whereby we are drawn toward the good (whether it is present or absent). Love is the principle and first emotion, without which no other emotion is possible.[3] Every emotion denotes either movement toward something or rest in something (desired). All emotions want to rest in the good, and this is also love for the good.

2. The goodness or evilness that we associate with emotions is based on *reason and will*—a judgment is made about the emotions, they are accepted (or rejected). So an emotion can be said to be voluntary either by "*being commanded by the reason and will, or from not being checked by the reason*

"Now whatever part the power of the soul takes in the act, follows apprehension. And the apprehension of the imagination, being a particular apprehension, is regulated by the apprehension of reason, which is universal; just as a particular active power is regulated by a universal active power. Consequently in this respect the act of the sensitive appetite is subject to the command of reason. On the other hand, condition or disposition of the body is not subject to the command of reason: and consequently in this respect, the movement of the sensitive appetite is hindered from being wholly subject to the command of reason.

"Moreover it happens sometimes that the movement of the sensitive appetite is aroused suddenly in consequence of an apprehension of the imagination of sense. And then such movement occurs without the command of reason: although reason could have prevented it, had it foreseen. Hence the Philosopher says (Polit. i, 2) that the reason governs the irascible and concupiscible not by a 'despotic supremacy,' which is that of a master over his slave; but by a 'politic and royal supremacy,' whereby the free are governed, who are not wholly subject to command."

3. *ST* I-II, q. 27, a. 4.

and will."[4] But in general, the emotions are automatic reactions and are not in themselves voluntary. They are, however, integrally related to voluntariness, as we shall see, and
that is why there are virtues (and vices) that govern the emotions themselves.

3. Emotions can increase or decrease the goodness or
evilness of an act.[5] Although it is more praiseworthy to do
a work of charity from the judgment of reason than from
the emotion of pity, the emotions can increase a good act by
resulting from the will's choice, as a sign of the intensity of
the will. I give my mother a present for her birthday with no
feelings accompanying the gift, or I give her a present with
my heart filled with love and gratitude. All else being equal,
the first scenario is still good (emotions are not necessary for

---

4. *ST* I-II, q. 24, a. 1: "We may consider the passions of the soul in two
    ways: first, in themselves; secondly, as being subject to the command
    of the reason and will. If then the passions be considered in them-
    selves, to wit, as movements of the irrational appetite, thus there is no
    moral good or evil in them, since this depends on the reason, as stated
    above. If, however, they be considered as subject to the command of
    the reason and will, then moral good and evil are in them. Because the
    sensitive appetite is nearer than the outward members to the reason
    and will; and yet the movements and actions of the outward members
    are morally good or evil, inasmuch as they are voluntary. Much more,
    therefore, may the passions, in so far as they are voluntary, be called
    morally good or evil. And they are said to be voluntary, either from
    being commanded by the will, or from not being checked by the will."

5. *ST* I-II, q. 24, a. 3. Note especially St. Thomas's example from Scrip-
    ture: "Accordingly just as it is better that man should both will good
    and do it in his external act; so also does it belong to the perfection of
    moral good, that man should be moved unto good, not only in respect
    of his will, but also in respect of his sensitive appetite; according to
    Psalm 83:3: 'My heart and my flesh have rejoiced in the living God':
    where by 'heart' we are to understand the intellectual appetite, and by
    'flesh' the sensitive appetite."

the act to be good), but the second scenario is more perfect because all the powers of the soul are integrated and united in the good.

4. In fact, the emotions belong to the perfection of moral goodness, by following right reason and will, and by being moved themselves toward the true good.

II. The Division of Emotions

The eleven emotions are divided into two categories, both categories rely on the distinction between attraction to good and aversion from evil, but the second category adds to these attractions the rational perception of "difficult."

1. Concupiscible: There are six concupiscible emotions, based on the simple desire for good and aversion to evil.

2. Irascible: There are five irascible emotions, based on the desire for good and aversion to evil with the added distinction that there is a perceived level of difficulty regarding the good or evil perceived.

The table on the following page shows the passions as grouped according to their proper objects (stimuli).

The concupiscible emotions respond to a simple good or evil. When a simple good is perceived (whether present or not), the emotion of *love* is experienced. When the simple good is absent, *desire* is the resulting emotion, and when the simple good is possessed, the emotion of *joy* results. Joy results from resting in the good obtained. It is when love is fulfilled.

When a simple evil is perceived, *hatred* is the resulting emotion. This is not willed hatred, which is sinful. This is the name for the emotion that naturally results from some simple evil (a bad odor, a sprained ankle, flunking a test). It has the psychological effect (or even physical effect) of

THE ELEVEN EMOTIONS

Concupiscible		Irascible	
Simple Good	Simple Evil	Difficult Good	Difficult Evil
Love	Hatred	Hope	Courage
Desire	Aversion	Despair	Fear
Joy	Sadness	[Joy]	Anger

making us withdraw from the evil. If the evil is not present, we experience *aversion*. If the evil is present, we experience the emotion of sorrow, or *sadness*. This can also happen due to a good lost (which is perceived as a present evil).

The irascible emotions respond to a difficult good or a difficult evil. Notice that this requires a judgment in the intellect. When a difficult good is perceived, and it is not yet attained but is perceived as possible to attain, the emotion of *hope* results. This is not the same as the virtue of hope, but is related. Hope gives us confidence in the face of obstacles and increases love and strengthens desire. When the difficult good that is not here yet is judged to be impossible to attain, the resulting emotion is *despair*. Again, this is not willed; it is a natural and psychological result of a judgment. It is interesting to note that despair regards a good. One cannot despair about an evil.

When a difficult evil is perceived, but is not here yet, and is judged as possible to overcome, the result is daring or *courage*. If the difficult evil, which is not here yet, is judged as impossible to overcome the resulting emotion is *fear*. And when the difficult evil is present, the resulting emotion is *anger*. There is no corresponding irascible emotion for when the difficult good is attained, because the emotion reverts to joy—which is for every perceived good that is attained.

Generally, the concupiscible emotions drive the inner sphere of man, and the irascible emotions give man the energy to stay alive, to endure or fight obstacles and to carry out necessary work in order to attain the good he desires.

The irascible emotions can be said to arise from the concupiscible, because they presuppose a desire for good and aversion for evil absolutely (which is the concupiscible).

In joy and sadness, all other emotions have their completion and end—they arise from all the other emotions.[6] This is because all other emotions have their movements in them: Movement begins in love, goes forward in desire, and ends in joy. With respect to evil, movement begins in hatred, goes on to aversion, and ends in sadness. Joy relates to the present good, sadness relates to present evil. Hope regards future good, and fear regards future evil.

Opposites can be regarding term (such as good or evil), and this can be found in the concupiscible emotions which regard good and evil absolutely, and also the irascible emotions. Since the irascible emotions consider the good and evil not absolutely, but under the aspect of difficulty, they can have another kind of opposition as well—that which regards approach or withdrawal from the same term. One exception is anger, which can have no

6.   *ST* I-II, q. 25, a. 4.

contrary regarding good or evil as its term, nor in regard to approach or withdrawal. Anger is caused by a difficult evil already present. Either it changes to sadness because it cannot overcome the evil, or it is relieved by some removal of the evil. Therefore, no movement of the soul is in itself contrary to anger. Anger is only overcome by removing the evil present in some way.

Fear is opposite of daring regarding the term; hope is contrary to despair regarding the term, hope is contrary to fear as regards good and evil; love and hatred, desire and aversion, joy or sadness, are all contraries in regard to good and evil as such.[7]

Some emotions result from a good or evil disposition of the person, and therefore are considered good or evil in themselves. Pity is when one is moved to a kind of love out of compassion for someone who is suffering (good). Shame is a kind of fear that involves a healthy assessment of one's guilt (good). Envy is sorrow at another's good (results from an evil disposition of the person, and therefore is considered evil).

Remember that truth is the key—joy is found when one achieves any good desired—so the thief finds joy when he finally steals the five million dollars. Even though that is the emotion of real joy, it is not ordered. It results from his evil disposition, and it is considered evil because of the disorder in the will and the lack of truth informing all the other powers.

It is better to direct the emotions toward whatever is good (Phil. 4:8) rather than suppress them or ignore them, or to constantly chide them for attraction to false

7.   *ST* I-II, q. 23, a. 4.

17

goods. The emotions themselves are neither good nor evil. Their purpose is to keep man alive. A person can never be "wrong" for having emotions. A person only commits evil when he wills what he knows is evil. The emotions are supposed to be integrated, so as to make a person rejoice more completely in the true good, and to reject more easily a true evil. Sometimes the emotions need to be overcome in order to achieve a true good, but that never means that the emotion itself is evil. It is only wounded, or disordered, and will eventually help to attain the true good if gently guided.

Remedies for sadness according to St. Thomas.

- Hot bath.
- Strong drink.
- Friendship.
- Study truth.

Remedies for anger according to St. Thomas.
- Humility.
- Play jokes.
- Feast, celebrate.
- Do something successful.
- Enjoy moderate pleasures (body and spirit), such as: a bath, drink, chocolate, food, etc.
- Friendship.
- Study the truth.
- Well-founded hope (review the reasons for Hope).
- Remember death.
- Forgiveness.
- Honesty.

- Prayer.
- Do good for another (acts of mercy).

III. Note on Repression

Every emotion is a response to an object, even if that object is another emotion. Because one and the same object can be considered as good, and therefore desirable, in one aspect, and evil or harmful in another aspect, more than one emotion can be aroused in regard to the same object. In fact, a whole series of emotions can be aroused; not only different emotions responding to the same object, but more emotions responding to those emotions. Although it is not impossible for them all to come under the guidance of reason and will, it sometimes happens that they compete or conflict with each other as well as with the will. The healthy resolution of these kinds of conflicts happens when the emotions are rightly subordinated to the intellect and will, such as when a diabetic chooses not to eat chocolate, when one takes unpleasant medicine to improve health, or when one undergoes surgery to preserve his life.[8] The virtuous man directs his emotions according to reason, sometimes making use of a suppression of the emotions in order to direct them to the

---

8. Conrad Baars, *Psychic Wholeness and Healing: Using All the Powers of the Human Psyche* (New York: Alba House, 1981), p.36: "Consequently, repression is impossible when there is a proper guidance by the intellect and will, nor can there be any question of a subsequent neurosis... It also follows from this that the rules of natural law, provided they are properly understood, can never exert a repressing action. For natural law teaches man how he should act according to reason in every circumstance. Hence, in the natural order moral acts correspond to reasonable acts, for if man is to attain the good that is proper to him, he must conduct himself as man, that is, as a rational being. By acting according to reason, his actions are morally right, because the rules of

true good, but not denying the emotion the space and time to run its natural course.[9]

The unhealthy resolution of these conflicts happens when the choice to deny an emotion its object is a truly good choice, but it is done in a harmful way simply by not acknowledging the emotion, or by not giving the emotion its "right" to respond to reality and run its bodily course. When one emotion overpowers a previously aroused emotion and squashes it down before the intellect and will have a chance to intervene, this is called *repression*.

In all cases of repression, the whole process "disables" the free choice by preventing the emotions from obtaining what they really need: the guidance of intellect and will. This neurotic repression deserves some attention in this section not only because these behaviors have a ramification on the relationship of the emotions with the free choice, but also because the incidence of its occurrence in recent decades seems to have increased drastically. Needless to say, whatever escapes the action of intellect and will cannot be willed and therefore cannot be considered moral, even if it appears to be very moral behavior, such as outbursts of anger, addictions to pornography, gambling, and other obsessive-compulsive behaviors.

The most common type (but not the only type) of repression is caused by an irascible emotion repressing a concupiscible emotion. Because it is the nature of the concupiscible

---

morality are merely formulations of what is intrinsically rational." One cannot claim, therefore, that it is repressive of itself to follow rules, especially the rules of natural law.

9. Allowing the bodily reaction is crucial for healthy development of the passions, such as crying, redness in the face, an increase in heart rate, a surge of energy, etc.

appetite to set in motion the irascible appetite, this kind of repression of a concupiscible emotion causes tension in the irascible emotions and leaves the concupiscible emotion "suspended in air," so to speak, because the object has been repressed. What is restrained is the action, not the emotion itself.[10] So the concupiscible emotions continue to react, and the irascible emotions continue to overtake them and repress them. When the repression is extreme, it renders the will helpless and leads to greater irritability and *excessive activity* for the utility appetite.[11] Classic examples are cases where fear or anger repress the sexual desire, where fear or courage repress anger, and where courage (sometimes called "energy") represses fear or sadness, or any unwanted emotion.

If a repressed person has grown up basing his beliefs and actions on his *felt* interpretations of moral teachings, he will have difficulty getting past the emotional reaction to those teachings. When he sees an attractive brunette, he will not allow himself to feel attracted, because he thinks this is wrong. If he lets his fear repress the desire he would normally have felt, he makes those desires inaccessible to reason, and the process goes on without relief:

> Because these emotions are buried alive, and are not dead and forgotten even though it may seem so for the moment, they try to rise up in order to get what they need: guidance by reason. However, as soon as they get close to the conscious level, fear is aroused

---

10. Conrad Baars, *Feeling and Healing Your Emotions*, ed. Suzanne M. Baars and Bonnie N. Shayne (Gainesville, FL: Bridge-Logos, 2003), p. 72.

11. Baars, *Psychic Wholeness and Healing*, p. 56.

and pushes them back again into the unconscious. The *battle between fear and desire* is on, and goes on without pause, only to break down sooner or later in life.[12]

This is the classic example of repressed emotion, which can begin in childhood or adulthood. Both the repressed emotion and the repressing emotion are in need of guidance by the intellect and will and are not able to obtain it.

The proper understanding of the concupiscible and irascible appetites makes it possible to attempt a healthy integration of the emotions. Although they have their own proper objects, the emotions still have a natural tendency to obey the will.[13] The virtuous life is a life that includes the emotions. Intellect, will, and emotions interact in harmony. Correct ordering of the sense appetites does not mean denigrating them to non-existence, as the ideal of the Stoics or Buddhists, but incorporating them in man's true and creative freedom, the virtuous use of all his faculties. For the voluntarist, "to will" means to be in control no matter how one feels.[14] To force the will in a repressive way clearly debilitates the will rather than makes full use of the real power of the will in desiring the true good. The emotions are intended not only for survival, but for obtaining the highest goods in life, which are to be ultimately enjoyed— friendship, truth, and God Himself. The highest goods are spiritual and intuitive, relating more appropriately to the pleasure appetite, which wants the good in itself. Hence, the

---

12. Baars, *Feeling and Healing*, p. 136.

13. Thomas Aquinas, *Questiones disputatae de Veritate*, q. 25, a. 3.

14. Baars, *Feeling and Healing*, p. 75.

importance of understanding the place of the emotions for every aspect of life.[15]

---

15. See Appendix II for more information about repression of emotions.

QUESTIONS

1. Why are the emotions also called passions? In your opinion, does our society see emotions as helpful or harmful? Give an example.

2. What are emotions and how do they come about? Identify emotions that you regularly experience. What seems to be their cause (when/why do they come about)?

3. How can the intellect and the will affect the emotions? Give an example from your own life of a time when your negative, or positive, thoughts about something has influenced your emotions.

4. Explain how love is the cause of the emotions. How might this love differ from love as a choice of the will?

5. If emotions are not bad in themselves, how is the goodness or evilness associated with the emotions to be determined?

Can the emotions influence the goodness or evilness of an act? Explain.

6. Why does anger not have a contrary emotion? If someone is angry, what might help them?

7. Is it wrong to feel any of the emotions? Are there bad emotions?

8. Oftentimes we feel guilty for our emotions. For example, sadness can be a cause of embarrassment and isolation. What are unhealthy ways that we try to deal with sadness? What are some healthy remedies?

9. What is repression of the emotions and how does it differ from subordination? Explain a situation when you have experienced (in yourself or in others) a repression and/or a subordination of the emotions.

10. What is the relationship between a healthy ordering of the emotions and freedom?

11. What does it mean to say that the emotions belong to the perfection of moral goodness? How do the emotions contribute to happiness on earth? In heaven?

APPLICATION

Have you ever encountered a topic about morality that angered or saddened you or a friend? Based upon this chapter, how would you counsel someone to subordinate the emotion (so that the conversation can continue) without repressing it?

APPLICATION

Think of the Puritan outlook on life as characterized by Nathaniel Hawthorne (*The Scarlet Letter*) and by H. L. Mencken ("Puritanism: the haunting fear that someone, somewhere, may be happy"). How might this Puritan suspicion of good emotions have affected our views of morality?

APPLICATION

B. J. Thomas, as Blue Swede in the soundtrack to the *Guardians of the Galaxy* (2014) recently reminded us, exalted the experience of being "hooked on a feeling." Human beings often struggle between the two extremes of denying emotions and being addicted to them. Can you think of any scenarios where you (or someone you know) have fallen into one of these extremes?

CHAPTER THREE

The Intellective Faculties

I. The Intellective Powers: Intellect and Will

1. The intellect is the faculty of soul by which we receive truth. The intellect desires truth, which is its object. The nature of the intellect is to know the essences of things (to receive them into itself). We are able to know. We are able to know that we know, think about thinking, we "abstract" ideas and think about them (for example, coldness, beauty, etc.). This is called *self-transcendence*. The proper operation of the intellect is to know, and the proper fulfillment of the operation of the intellect is to know the truth. The ultimate object of the intellect is to know the (true) essence of all causes, which is God's essence.

The intellect has three proper operations:

- Abstraction.
- Judgment.
- Reasoning.

2. The will is the rational appetite, the spiritual faculty by which we desire the good. The nature of the will is to desire the good, and to move toward it (with the aim of being united to the good somehow appropriately). The will desires good and the end, its object. For example: health. The will desires anything that is seen as good, and desires it as an end (either in itself, or as a means to the end). The will is both active and passive. It is moved by the good, desires or rests in the good, and moves itself (and the other powers) toward the good.

The nature of the will is not "domineering", as in the imposition or commanding action of something to be done or resisted, but the nature of the will is rather "unitive"—the will wants to be united with the good.[1]

The proper operation of the will is twofold:

---

1. Servais Pinckaers, O.P., *The Sources of Christian Ethics*, trans. Sr. Mary Thomas Noble, O.P. (Washington, DC: Catholic University of America Press, 1995), pp. 389–90: "[T]he will was primarily the faculty of love and desire. These were its first two acts, according to the treatise on the passions (*ST* I-II, q. 25, a. 2). At the origin of the voluntary movement there existed a spiritual spontaneity, an attraction to the good. Only following this did the will act upon itself and move itself to will those ways and means leading to the good it loved. This was effected precisely by an act of choice. One could speak of the will as imposing itself only in the case of some resistance to be overcome. This could be interior, issuing from our sensibility, or exterior, on the part of others. In every case the spontaneity of love and desire was primary and animated the will's other acts. The will was therefore not a 'pressure,' but it gave rise to an 'impression' of goodness, which caused the attraction... The outcome of the voluntary movement would be the pleasure or joy resulting from union with the good. Its fullness was happiness. The will was therefore not domineering by nature but unitive."

- To desire the good.
- To delight (rest) in the good (be united to it.)

Notice that the nature of the will is *not* to choose. To choose is an act of intellect and will together; it is metaphysically impossible for this to be the nature of the will, as we shall see.

Now, we often think of the will as the "mover," and it is by way of desiring that the will moves and is moved. But in order to *act*, the will requires the operation of the intellect. The will never moves on its own (as if it could move against the intellect). Movement of the soul (whether interior or exterior) is always an act of both intellect and will together.

3. Interaction of the powers.

A. The combined operation of the will with the intellect is *to choose*, with its ultimate fulfillment being to choose the true good.

B. The intellect can never act *without* the will, and the will can never act *without* the intellect. The intellect and the will *can never act against each other*. It is not possible to make a human act (even one that is only interior) by intellect alone, or by will alone. It is metaphysically impossible for the intellect and the will to "disagree" or "fight" or, worst of all, act separately. After examining the interaction of the two faculties, this will become more clear.

C. It is absolutely incorrect to say that the intellect perceives the good, and the will chooses it. The will never, never, never chooses anything without the combined operation of the intellect. The proper operation of the will is to desire and to delight. However, the will cannot "rest" or find true happiness, or find its proper fulfillment, in a false good. The will can only be satisfied by a true good.

Herein lies morality. A false good can only give the will a "false rest."

D. The combined operation of intellect and will in choosing (a good) is called *free choice* (in Latin, *liberum arbitrium*). This is the nature of *human freedom*.

4. Influences on the will.

Any object apprehended as good will move the will. The will can be moved directly or indirectly from exterior stimuli or interior stimuli.

A. *The (external) influence of the emotions on the intellect and will.* Any object which is apprehended as good will cause the emotion of desire (or love), and anything apprehended as evil will cause the emotion of aversion (or hatred). The emotions are psychic responses to exterior and interior stimuli. Their response to good and evil will influence the will toward or away from good and evil objects, without making any choice necessary. Their mechanism is necessary for survival, but does not always correspond to the truth about reality. For example, the emotion of anger can cause one to want revenge, and thus to seek an evil act, which is seen as good because it will assuage the desire for revenge (this aspect of the act is seen as good, and can become exaggerated). The emotion of sadness can cause one to fail to do something good because there will be some aspect of sadness or hardship involved in doing the good. The emotions of themselves are neutral, neither good nor evil, but are meant to be used for good, and meant to share in the goodness of free choice. But virtue is necessary for the emotions to be trained to follow the rational nature. We must always accept the emotion, but we do not always have to act on it. It is in this way that the emotions move the will indirectly, by influencing the judgment of the intellect, and swaying the will in its desiring.

B. *The will can move itself.* Remember that the first act of the will is by nature to desire whatever is good. As soon as something is desired, one sees that there will be some *means* necessary to obtain that good, and here the will moves itself—that is, according to the means for reaching the end. By the act of willing the end (the good desired), the will moves itself to will the means, even if the end is not always consciously thought: I want to go to Florida. I do not have to be thinking about Florida (willing to go there) consciously during the whole trip. Nonetheless, I am aware that the reason for the trip is to go to Florida, even if I make a detour, stop and enjoy other goods, etc. Everything is done because I want to go to Florida—I will the end and all the means necessary to achieve it.

C. *The intellect moves the will, by presenting the true good to it.* The will relies on the intellect for the perception of every good. "The intellect rules the will, not by inclining it to that to which it tends, but by showing it that to which it should tend,"[2] which is seen and desired rationally as an end. If one never has a concept of chocolate, one cannot desire chocolate. If one thinks that it is truly good to kill one's enemy, then he will desire to kill his enemy. If one thinks that it is evil to kill one's enemy, then he will struggle to resist the temptation to kill his enemy. Truth drives our desires. We naturally want the truth, and become angry if someone lies to us. When the intellect is enlightened by faith, this ignites the will to desire even more truths that come from God, truths that really set us free, truths that inspire and give courage, until we discover that truth is a Person. And we desire that Person more and more. Knowledge fuels the desire.

---

2. *De Veritate*, q. 22, a. 11, ad 5.

THE MOVEMENTS OF THE WILL

The will is moved by:

1. Itself
2. Intellect   ➤   DIRECTLY
3. God (grace)

4. Emotion
5. Bodily dispositions
6. Senses
7. Interior powers   ➤   INDIRECTLY
8. Personal virtues and vices
9. Other people
10. Events, environment, situations

The intellect, in presenting to the will the good in all its aspects, adds the important element of this act's relation to a man's final end.[3]

D. *Only God can move the will, as something outside the will.* God moves the will as its Creator. As universal cause, and also by grace, God can move our will. How does this not affect our freedom? Because true freedom is the ability

---

3. For example, upon the smell of pasta, the concupiscible appetite will have a craving for fettuccini alfredo because the taste is pleasant, it satisfies the body's hunger, is accompanied by pleasant memories, and the like. The will, not denying all of these goods, desires the fettuccini alfredo for all of the same reasons (which are good), with the additional judgment, after consultation with the intellect, that this desire, in all of these aspects, is reasonable here and now, contributing to the good of his life, and in accord with man's final end (or at least not against it) and is therefore a good choice, and commands the carrying out of obtaining and eating the pasta.

to choose what is truly good. If God helps us do that, then He is helping us become more free—not obstructing our freedom. God moves everything according to its nature—whether voluntary or not.

E. *All other stimuli move the will indirectly.* They do this with or through the emotions or through the intellect, or through the will itself (by habits that surround the will, strengthening or weakening the will with regard to goods perceived and evils hated). Virtues and vices, whether residing in the intellect, will, or emotions, influence the will indirectly.

II. Summary

The proper operation of the will is *not* to choose (this is an operation of intellect and will together), but to desire [the good], and to delight in the possession of that good. Other animals act according to instinct, but humans are supposed to act according to reason, and freely act according to reason while integrating their whole being, which requires the body and emotions (not like Dr. Spock). *Real* freedom is not just the ability to choose, but the ability to choose in such a way that one's nature is fulfilled—that is, to choose something that will bring man true happiness. Freedom must *include* the ability to know. That is why the will is often called the intellective (or rational) appetite. The only thing that can satisfy our desire for infinite truth, infinite goodness, infinite beauty, is God Himself. He is the good, the ultimate good that will never end.

Questions

1. What is the intellect? What is its function?

2. What is the will? What is its function?

3. How do the intellect and will work together to choose? How is choice not simply a function of the will (i.e., how is it that neither the intellect nor the will ever act alone)?

4. "If loving you is wrong, then I don't want to be right," country singer Barbara Mandrell stated (*Moods*, 1978). What conflict between intellect, will, and emotions is set up in this situation? How would you respond?

5. What is the nature of human freedom? How does this understanding of freedom illuminate the meaning of Saint Augustine's statement: "The good man is free, even if he is a slave; the evil man is a slave, even if he is a king" (*City of God*, IV.3)?

6. List and explain the various influences or "movers" of the will. Of which one are you most aware in your own life (i.e., "what moves you")? Of which one are you least aware? Why is this level of self-reflection difficult?

7. What is true freedom? What is required for true freedom?

8. Why is true freedom difficult to attain?

APPLICATION

Explain a scenario when morality seemed like a rule and something that limited your freedom. How might a better explanation of the truth, or a better disposition (openness) on your part have made the truth appear freeing and appealing rather than oppressive and burdensome?

APPLICATION

What strikes you most about the following meditation from Saint Augustine?

> Show me one who is full of longing, one who is hungry, one who is a pilgrim and suffering from thirst in the desert of this world, eager for the fountain in the homeland of eternity; show me someone like that, and he knows what I mean... You have only to show a leafy branch to a sheep, and it is drawn to it. If you show nuts to a boy, he is drawn to them. He runs to them because he is drawn, drawn by love, drawn without any physical compulsion, drawn by a chain attached to his heart. "Everyone is drawn by his own desire."

This is a true saying, and earthly delights and pleasures, set before those who love them, succeed in drawing them. If this is so, are we to say that Christ, revealed and set before us by the Father, does not draw us? What does the soul desire more than truth? (*Tractates on Saint John*, 26, 4–6: *CCL* 36, 261–263; emphasis added)

CHAPTER FOUR

True Human Freedom

I. The Nature of Human Freedom

To choose is a kind of conclusion.[1] The will regards the end as universal, and choosing is about the means to an end. Moral choices are not about the obedience of one's will to the command of reason, but about the creative capacity to go for the good perceived. The will does not exert energy to overcome the judgment of the intellect (this is called voluntarism). The powers of intellect and will *unite* to form *one principle* for action in every choice, whether interior or exterior.

Notice that the will is *not free* with regard to its *nature*—on the *level of its being*, the will *of necessity* desires the good, under the aspect of a universal. The will desires whatever is good. The will is *determined* to the good (not determined *by* the good). The will *is free* with regard to its choice (which requires the cooperation of the intellect), not with regard to its nature, and this is what we normally consider when we consider human freedom, the freedom to choose with regard to particular choices.

The will naturally wills good, but not any particular good.[2] This liberty concerns whether one chooses tea or coffee, as well as whether or not any particular act is in conformity with the love of God. When the intellect presents a good object to the will, the will is not forced. Even if the intellect has made no mistake about the object's goodness, the choice will still be free because any particular good is not good in every possible way. The will does not tend toward any particular good in an absolute way. The way in which the good is lacking in perfection will have a different reception according to the disposition of the will. One person will prefer pleasure over fame, another will not be tempted by money, another will want power at all costs, etc., and all of these for intellectual, habitual, and emotional reasons.[3] These particular goods are desirable under the aspect of some end which is not the final end, and therefore do not move the will necessarily, but only according to that aspect of good which is being considered.

Human freedom is found in the fact that the intellect and will are not determined of necessity to *any particular good*. This implies that the human person has freedom to choose between particular goods (as means to an end—happiness), and this requires the collaboration of the intellect. This is the concept behind the modern understanding of

---

1. Daniel Westberg, *Right Practical Reason: Aristotle, Action, and Prudence in Aquinas* (Oxford: Clarendon Press, 1994), p. 89. Choice is called a kind of conclusion because it involves the judgment, sometimes called the decision or discrimination or *judicio*, of the intellect. In speculative matters, intellectual discourse comes to a conclusion, and in practical matters discourse comes to a conclusion with choice.

2. *De Veritate*, q. 22, a. 6, ad 5.

3. Westberg, *Right Practical Reason*, p. 93.

"free will." However, in St. Thomas's view, this concept is called *liberum arbitrium*.

II. *Liberum arbitrium*[4]

Liberum arbitrium is the capacity for freedom in man. This capacity for freedom, in which the intellect and will function together, is central for the image of God in man. The ability to have power over one's acts is the primary way in which man imitates the nature and power of God. It is a spiritual capacity, manifested in this world through man's actions. According to St. Bernard of Clairvaux, "free choice is the most powerful thing this side of God."[5]

Liberum arbitrium is not a habit, but is rather a capacity, even though the *liberum arbitrium* is conditioned by habits, such as the virtues (or vices) and the gifts of the Holy Spirit.

---

4. "As used by Aquinas, the term is understood to refer to the joint action of the intellect and will in the exercise of freedom. The term is not limited to Aquinas, but was used with this precise meaning during Aquinas's time and before. It happened after Aquinas that 'there was a growing tendency to put the emphasis on the will as the decisive factor, until *liberum arbitrium* largely became synonymous with free will'" (Westberg, *Right Practical Reason*, p. 81).

   The translation of *liberum arbitrium* as "free will" instead of "free choice" to this day indicates the continuation of that voluntarist interpretation. I am not using the term "free will" in order to avoid this connotation. I use the translation of "free choice" with the understanding that *liberum arbitrium* is the capacity for free choice which involves the combined activity of intellect and will. Although the word "choice" is tainted with an absolutist mentality, especially due to the separation of truth from freedom in contemporary use, the defining reference to the intellect and the modifier "free" distinguish it from *electio* as well as preserve it from the voluntaristic interpretation. For this reason it is sometimes translated as "free judgment," but I refrain from that translation because it seems to put more emphasis on the intellect.

5. *De Veritate*, q. 22, a. 9, *sed contra* 1.

A habit is a quality by which a faculty is inclined to act. To judge does not require the addition of any habit, but is the proper act of a reasonable nature. "Similarly, what is added in the adverb *freely* does not exceed the scope of the power, for something is said to be done freely inasmuch as it is in the power of the one doing it."[6] "Freely" denotes the power itself, and is not a habit modifying choice.

Liberum arbitrium is not a separate faculty from intellect and will, but is rather the combination of these two faculties in their action of choice. It is the term for the two faculties working together as one power. The intellect and will have a creative interplay throughout any decision, whether it concerns the color for a tablecloth, what gift to give someone, or how to carry out certain burdensome tasks. Incidentally, the Holy Spirit does not mind being invited into mundane choices like these, but rather seems to delight in inspiring man in his daily choices by elevating his natural faculties, removing obstacles, giving him new ideas, and assisting him with grace in the training of his will.

The whole cause of freedom is rooted in the cognition of, and desire for, the universal good. *Liberum arbitrium* refers to the joint action of the reason and the will, mutually and creatively influencing one another as they adapt and react to the influences coming from within the human being and from without. Just as a man perceives things according to the type of man he is, so he responds with his freedom according to his unique disposition and perception. In the mature man freedom of choice results in creativity, allowing for his unique response to God and the inner promptings of the Holy Spirit.

---

6. *De Veritate*, q. 24, a. 4.

Liberum arbitrium in its perfection consists in the perfect knowledge and perfect love of the true and the good, with no possibility of error or end. This is how God's will is perfectly free. To be free, then, cannot mean to have the ability to choose evil. To be perfectly free means to will the true good completely and forever. Man's freedom, however, has the ability to fail.

The fact that man needs grace does not negate the faculty of free choice. This is seen by the fact that one who does not have grace can still choose the good, and one who has grace can still choose evil. Man's freedom of choice is weakened by sin, but never wholly lost.[7]

Servais Pinckaers gives the example of a pianist who needs the training and practice of learning how to play correctly in order to become *free* to be creative in making beautiful music come forth from the instrument.[8] All human faculties need training (i.e., discipline, practice, development) in order to perform their proper functions. The same is true of the soul. According to Aquinas, we are not born free. True spiritual liberty must grow. And it grows precisely by making free and creative acts. With the guidance of faith and the natural attraction to good, man must reflect on the truth which will set him free.

III. Grace and Free Choice

Grace can be considered in a broad sense as "the very mercy of God by which He interiorly moves the mind and arranges external conditions for man's salvation."[9] In this

---

7. *De Veritate*, q. 24, a. 1, ad 11; *De Veritate*, q. 24, a. 4, ad 6 and ad 7.

8. Pinckaers, *Sources of Christian Ethics*, pp. 354–55.

9. *De Veritate*, q. 24, a. 14.

sense, grace is not considered as a habitual gift, as being in the state of sanctifying grace, but as God's merciful action in the circumstances of man's life as well as His interior gifts and inspirations.

Grace does not abrogate the freedom of man, but rather strengthens it so that man can more easily choose and adhere to the true good.

The fact that man can be an instrument of God does not exclude the notion of having the capability of free choice, because nothing prevents an instrument from being moved as well as being able to move itself.[10] This concept is disconcerting for the modern voluntarist who considers any help to be an infringement on his autonomy. However, Aquinas insists, if freedom means choosing and adhering to the true good, then grace is necessary for the *liberum arbitrium* to consistently and permanently act according to its nature. The perfection of it only exists in heaven. Therefore, *the blessed in heaven are the most free*, for they are confirmed in grace. They cannot choose evil; their wills permanently, and without fear of failing, are united to the true Good.

Maturation in freedom requires a kind of transformation of both reason and will.[11] Grace corrects the functioning of the intellect and will and heals the disorder caused by sin, so that the will can more spontaneously and firmly tend toward true goods. Man can become more and more free, with God's help, transformed from within. True freedom requires training of the mind and the will in the virtues,

---

10. *De Veritate*, q. 24, a. 1, ad 5.

11. Wojciech Giertych, O.P., "Conscience and the *Liberum Arbitrium*," in *Crisis of Conscience*, ed. John M. Haas (New York: The Crossroad Publishing Company, 1996), p. 67.

which result in peace when the true good attracts the will without being hampered by apparent goods, and joy when the true good is creatively chosen. "A mind that is open to a living God is open to the enriching novelty of truth,"[12] and rejoices in the creative response of love that is called forth from him. When obstacles that block the harmony of intellect and will, such as fear, concupiscence, and pride, are healed by grace, charity can flower in the soul and allow the natural hunger for creativity to develop into true liberty.

We have seen that there are two levels in willing. One is determined by nature, and provides man with a necessary and natural attraction to what is good. On the level of attraction only, there is no merit because it is not freely chosen. However, when man's acts are ordered to this true end, he merits by striving to be united with God, his true happiness. In this way, Aquinas says a man can merit "by willing what he wills necessarily."[13]

To explain this, Aquinas gives a comparison between the way God has provided for animals and the way God has provided for man. For their bodies, animals have been provided with everything they need, such as covering, tools, and the like, whereas man is not provided with these things since he has reason in order to provide for himself with creativity. Furthermore, man can receive inspiration from God in man's intellect, will, and even emotions, spurring man on to the true good in providing for himself and others. In regard to apprehension, animals are provided with a natural instinct for self-preservation and protection, whereas man has implanted in him universal principles from which he is

---

12. Ibid., p. 72.

13. *De Veritate*, q. 22, a. 7, *sed contra* 2.

supposed to be able to draw conclusions that are necessary for him to survive. In regard to their appetites also animals are drawn to what suits their nature, whereas with man there is a distinction to be made. "[M]an has implanted in him an appetite for his last end in general so that he naturally desires to be complete in goodness. But in just what that completeness consists, whether in virtues or knowledge or pleasure or anything else of the sort, has not been determined for him by nature."[14] So it is then, that with the help of grace, when man knows and wills that which is truly good for him, he merits, not because he desires happiness in general, which he naturally desires, but because he desires the vision of God as his final end, or a particular good that is in accord with that end, by his own free willing. When his choice is specified to this or that particular good, then he merits or demerits.[15]

The consequence of merit or demerit shows that man is responsible for what he chooses, even what he chooses to desire. It must be in his power to will something which deserves blame or merit; otherwise there could be no blame or merit. In order for man to merit when he chooses that to which he has the deepest inclination, there must be freedom involved in that choice. This requires grace. Grace does not replace our ability to merit, but rather makes it possible for us to merit. "Merit and demerit are in some sense situated in the will... But...no one becomes a sinner except by himself;

---

14. *De Veritate*, q. 22, a. 7.

15. Ibid. "[I]f anyone were by erroneous reasoning to be brought to desire as his happiness some particular good—for example, bodily pleasures, in which his happiness does not in fact consist—he incurs demerit by so desiring. This is not because he desires happiness, but because he unwarrantedly desires as his happiness this particular thing in which his happiness is not found."

nor does anyone become just except by the operation of God and his own cooperation."[16] How then does man accept the operation of God into his own will? How can man's will and God's will perform the same act?

Grace is not some external help that gives man the power to do whatever he wants. Grace is the interior transforming action of the Holy Spirit that unites man to God by strengthening man's power to more fully desire and easily choose that which is truly good.

Even just a small effort on the part of man draws down the grace of God, who sees what is done in the secret of the heart. The man who sees his need for God is much more likely to ask for the help that he needs and make room for God to work than the man who does not know his own need for God's grace. The removal of obstacles is one of the main tasks for free choice in order to prepare for grace.

IV. God's Will in Relation to Man's Will

Since the will is a natural thing, God can work in it just as He can work in nature. Just as the will can change or move itself due to its nature, so can God change or move it. There are two ways in which God can change the will. As Creator, God can change the will from the point of view of the will itself, and also from the point of view of the will's object. From the point of view of the will itself, only God can work inside the will in order to change it, and this He can do in two ways:

- By simply moving it, and
- By introducing a form into the will itself.

16. *De Veritate*, q. 22, a. 9, *sed contra* 2.

When God moves the will simply,

> He causes an inclination to succeed a previous inclination so that the first disappears and the second remains. Accordingly, that to which He induces the will is not contrary to an inclination still extant but merely to one that was previously there. This is not, then, violence or force.[17]

For example, with a simple prayer such as, "Thy will be done, not mine," one is asking for this very grace. By willing that his own will be changed, man invites God to change it. God can incline a man's will to want His will rather than the man's own will. Even still, God can do such a thing without a prayer on man's part. As the first agent of the will, God can change man's will to want something that he simply did not want before, with or without "the addition of any habit."[18] Furthermore, sometimes God ordains that such graces only be given if requested.

God makes our will like His own will first of all by its being, that is, by being in His image (the fact that the will desires goodness), and second by its likeness, that is, in its acts which are good insofar as man, through his intellect and will with the help of grace, chooses what is truly good.[19] Knowing this makes man responsible for cooperating with

---

17. *De Veritate*, q. 22, a. 8.

18. Ibid.

19. When it is sometimes said that God inclines a man to evil (as in the case of Pharaoh in the Old Testament), this is to be understood in the sense that God can withhold grace for His own divine purposes, so that the man's heart does incline toward evil. But in no way should it be understood that God inclines one to evil. See ibid.

grace in order to conform his will to God's will, that is, to want what God wants, to love what God loves, especially and finally to know and love God Himself and be united with Him. *To conform* implies that something is moving toward conformity with the other thing, which is the primary thing desired.[20] There is nothing volitional about the conformity of man's will to God's will on the part of the image, on the part of its nature. But there is a conformity that is volitional on the part of man's freely chosen acts. We are held to conform our wills to God's will in proportion to the knowledge that we have.[21] This will become clearer when we study the nature of the human act itself.

When God introduces a form into the will itself, this is a quality which strengthens the will toward the good, what we usually call virtue.

Just as it is not inconsonant with air that it be illuminated, but merely that by its own nature it cannot be luminous, so it is not inconsonant with *liberum arbitrium* that it be confirmed in good by grace, as are the blessed in heaven.

V. The Possibility of Failure

Then how is it possible that the will is still able to reject something that the intellect presents as good? As long as the good presented is an imperfect good, there will be some aspect of non-good in it. And so the will is not determined to desire any *particular* good. A particular good can never be the Absolute Good. Hence the need for deliberation. The will wills that the intellect consider aspects of goodness in things, and the intellect works at finding the truth about

---

20. *De Veritate*, q. 23, a. 7, ad 11.

21. *De Veritate*, q. 23, a. 7, ad 1.

the thing in question. For various reasons (malice, weakness, concupiscence, emotion) the will can be less attracted to a true good, or even fail altogether to desire a true good. This is how falsehood, emotion, and sin can weaken the will's desire for good. But we know the definition of sin, and the experience of it—where it seems that the will "goes against" reason. For something to be a sin, it is required that the agent know it is wrong and still choose it. Indeed, it is not a sin if the agent does not know that the choice is wrong. So how does it happen?

How can it happen that the will and intellect fail to choose the true good that is known? St. Thomas says that either an emotion, or the malicious intent of the agent, causes him to will that the intellect *not* consider the truth that it knows about this particular act. The will moves the intellect to fail to apply truth to a situation here and now. The famous example is that of the adulterer who, in his emotion, wills that the intellect *not* apply the truth that he believes (that adultery is wrong) to this particular situation, and so commits the act. It would not be possible to commit the act without the intellect's compliance. Therefore, the weak or malicious will can prevent the intellect from working well. And this is precisely what we experience. Hence the need for practice in desiring what is truly good, especially in the face of temptation, arduousness, and other difficulties.

Now, in the case of failing to choose the true good, the principles are the same. The intellect and the will cooperate in every free choice. When faced with the choice for God Himself (say friendship with God, or the final choice to be united with God in heaven), how can one fail to choose the absolutely true Good? If St. Thomas's theory be taken as correct, then one cannot fail to desire the absolutely true good, which has no imperfection. Thomas answers that even when faced with the absolute, perfect, universal Good Himself, *the choice remains a particular choice* for this particular agent at this particular moment, and the possibility of failure holds. One man might fail because the choice seems impossible to him for some reason (intellect and/or emotions influence his perception of the true Good), or one man might fail because the choice seems too arduous (habits of sloth or gluttony influence the will). Even when faced with the universal good, the choice is particular. All the habits of intellect and will leading up to this final choice, when we see God face to face, will make it either easier or harder to make.

It is the rational aspect of the will that makes it open to opposites,[22] but not able to will evil directly. The fact that the will can tend toward evil is not freedom, but merely a *sign* of freedom, belonging to the indetermination of the will regarding the means to the end. "[T]he ability of the will to be directed to evil does not come from the fact of its being from God but from that of its being made out of nothing."[23] Having been made out of nothing, the will lacks something. This is not against its nature, nor is it a sign of a corrupt nature. All created things lack something, that is, their end. While man tries to achieve his true end, especially with a darkened intellect and the influence of lower appetites not always following reason, it is not surprising that mistakes are made. In fact, it seems that God expected this to happen and planned the remedy from all eternity.

The modern misunderstanding of freedom is actually

---

22. *De Veritate*, q. 22, a. 5, *sed contra* 5.

23. *De Veritate*, q. 22, a. 6, ad 3.

not a modern idea. It dates back to William of Ockham from the thirteenth century. A brilliant treatment of the history of this idea has been written by Father Servais Pinckaers, a Belgian Dominican who was instrumental in crafting the moral section of the *Catechism of the Catholic Church* published in 1992. Rather than summarize the history itself, I have taken the summary of his conclusion from his book *Sources of Christian Ethics* in chart form[24] and made my own variation:

FREEDOM ACCORDING TO OCKHAM AND ST. THOMAS AQUINAS

Freedom of Indifference

Freedom for Excellence

The power to choose between contraries (to be able to choose between good and evil).

The power to choose what is truly good. The choice of evil denotes a lack of freedom.

Freedom resides in the will alone.

The nature of the will is to be able to choose (free will), and the proper operation of the will is to choose.

Freedom is the combined action of intellect and will, requiring truth and good. The nature of the will is to desire the good, which must be shown by the intellect.

1. Natural inclinations are not included in the nature of freedom. Freedom is indifferent with regard to natural inclinations.

1. Freedom is rooted in the natural inclinations to the true and the good. It springs from a natural attraction to what appears to be true and good.

24. Pinckaers, *Sources of Christian Ethics*, p. 350.

2. A human being is either free or not free. There is no middle ground between being free and not being free.

2. Freedom must develop through exercise and education. Growth in freedom is essential for human perfection.

3. Freedom is exercised perfectly in each free choice. Each act is independent, isolated from other acts, and is performed at the instant the decision is made.

3. True freedom integrates all actions in view of an end, which united the actions interiorly (by intention).

4. There is no need for virtue to help one to become more free. There are no habits which can influence freedom. There is no inherent finality regarding freedom. For a believing Christian, the highest virtue becomes obedience, and all of morality is seen in light of obeying God or not.

4. Virtue is essential for true freedom. Finality is a principle element of free action, where habits are necessary. Charity, love for the true good, is the highest virtue and binds the rest together.

5. Law is an external restraint to freedom. Law is a limit for freedom and creates an irreducible tension with freedom.

5. Law is a necessary external aid to development in freedom, together with the natural inclination toward the true and the good. Law is an ordinance of reason, helping human action to conform to objective truth. It is especially necessary in the first stages of education, to help with progress in virtue.

6. Freedom is a matter of will, and therefore can be the cause

6. Freedom is open and inclusive of the whole personality, where

of the will's separation from the other faculties (like the intellect and natural inclinations). Therefore one human being's freedom need not relate to anyone else's freedom.

the intellect and will operate together with all the lower faculties. Individual freedom has a necessary connection with the common good and growth in virtue of society.

7. The resulting moral theory is one based on obligation or law as the source for limiting one's freedom to choose. Scripture is read with a focus on moral absolutes as the only directive for human action.

7. The resulting moral theory centers on the natural desire for happiness as the finality that drives the faculties to their proper ends, focusing on the virtues as the habits which direct them to the true good and the necessity of grace. All of Scripture contributes to growth in the moral life, which is seen in light of the desire for God and God's desire for a relationship with man.

VI. The Interplay Between the Intellect and the Will in the Act of Choice

Aquinas has twelve steps going back and forth between intellect and will for a free choice. But we only insist on three or four: *intention*, *deliberation* (if needed), *decision*, and *execution*. In any case, it is clear that the intellect and the will move each other—I must will to think, and my thinking moves the will. However, we cannot say that the process goes on indefinitely, and it must have had a beginning. The very first movement of the will—that of desiring the good—does not depend on the intellect *per se*. You do not have to tell yourself to desire goodness. (Here goodness means anything desirable. Even when someone desires to steal, he desires it under some aspect of good.) But after that first movement (which is one of nature, and so we say that it is given by God), the will must move the intellect to investigate what is the true good.[25] Together the intellect and will move the agent to his true end (the good). The intellect and will act together in each of the above steps, even though it seems that at times one predominates. Then the final act of the will is one of resting, or delighting in the good possessed. Man's final end is not in "choosing" *per se*. Choosing is man's *means* to his *end*. Man's end is delighting forever in the true good obtained.

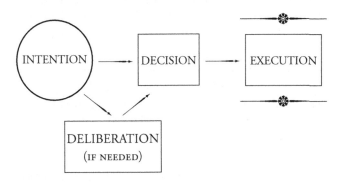

This is further shown in that if man's true happiness (end) consisted in the *act of choosing*, then all eternity would be spent *choosing* (which implies that something is desired, which implies that something is lacking…), and this cannot be eternal happiness.

---

25. This is the "truth about the good" to which Pope St. John Paul II refers throughout his encyclical *Veritatis Splendor* (1993), the first papal encyclical regarding moral theology itself.

We must consider the secondary aspect of the will, the fact that particular choices are free and undetermined, not in order to be contrary to the underlying nature of the will, but in order to perfect the faculties of intellect and will in their cooperative choices toward the true good. It is the most important aspect in the sense that here is where man makes himself to be good or evil, and therefore happy or miserable, by his freely chosen actions, by his freely chosen desires. But if he understands the underlying nature of his own freedom as, "I want to be free to do whatever I want, to choose whatever I want, to desire whatever I want," he will be frustrated by his own nature. If man understands his own freedom to consist in wanting the truth and the good, then he has a chance to direct his actions toward happiness and freedom. He may in this way open himself to grace, even unknowingly. The absolute good is what he wants, but is not an option to him. He must take steps toward it. The goods open to him are imperfect, contingent, means to the end, and not the end itself. He must choose.

This metaphysical freedom is the freedom of the will in its very passivity. Because there is no absolute good except God, the will relies on the intellect to present lesser goods, and to specify a particular good for the will to desire. But the will is not forced to desire it. The intellect is not alone in its search; the will helps by its right desire. The will is not alone in its desiring; the intellect helps by its ordering and comparing and deducing. This does not put all of the stress on the will as the "chooser," nor does it leave all choice to the judgment of reason. Simply it underlines the fact that the two faculties always work together, in every judgment, in every choice, in every desire. In order for something to move and be moved, there must be something immobile underlying it,[26] and this is precisely the natural tendency of the intellect toward the true and the natural tendency of the will toward the good. These are the immovable tendencies which give purpose and possibility to man's freedom, his freedom to receive and react to a good.

1. Powers are ordered to their proper objects:

- The power of sight is ordered to (aims at) the object of color (this is what that power is made to be able to receive).
- The power of hearing is ordered to receiving sound.
- The power of touch is ordered to sensitive reception (pressure, textures, cold).
- The power of the intellect is ordered to truth.
- The power of the will is ordered to the good.

2. Acts move the power to its object (and these acts can be more or less deliberate):

- The act of opening my eyes moves the eyes to see color.
- The act of eating food results in digestion (although digestion is not deliberate, eating is).
- The act of imagining (and all of the above) results in my senses somehow responding— usually emotionally and physically.
- The act of reasoning results in knowledge, and should result in the acquisition of truth.

---

26. *ST* I, q. 79, a. 8, *corpus*; *ST* I, q. 82, a. 1, *corpus*.

- The act of desiring should result in some connection with good (movement toward the good, at least interiorly).
- The act of willing can be of two kinds:
  - Elicited: Proceeds immediately from the will itself, such as love or desire.
  - Commanded: Proceeds from some other power, but under the command of the will—such as to walk, to speak, etc. (sometimes called *imperated*).

Virtues are those habits of soul which help us to quickly and with facility choose the true good and avoid a true evil (resist a false good). Certain virtues will strengthen certain powers (the emotions, the intellect and will). This is why virtue is necessary for true happiness. It is not so much that virtue is an end in itself, but virtue supplies the needed aid for the perfection of the powers.

VII. Erroneous Opinions Regarding Freedom

Because the wise man must not only seek to know the truth about things, but must also be able to distinguish the truth from falsehoods that resemble it, we must also seek to distinguish true freedom from erroneous concepts of freedom.

All theories of freedom have an underlying idea of the nature of the will and its relationship with the intellect. Erroneous opinions can be thus categorized according to each one's view of these two faculties of the soul.

1. The wrong type of exaltation of freedom.

A. *Intellectualism.* If the intellect perceives the truth about an object, and then the will desires it automatically, this places all of the importance on the intellect for moral action. The prime mover is then seen as the practical intellect, seeing the truth, and the will is either obedient or disobedient to the truth perceived. This is the misguided intellectualist interpretation of Aquinas, which has resulted in the over-emphasis on conscience, and the over-dependence on the moralistic manuals that the past three centuries have witnessed. In its over-emphasis on the role of the intellect, this position results in an under-developed idea of the nature of the will and its interplay with the intellect. Ironically, the highest virtue becomes obedience, even if blind. This position is seen today in those who have an insatiable desire to know things, even truths in theology, thinking that this will make them good.

B. *Pelagianism*. Pelagius, in his effort to defend free choice, taught that man is able to avoid sin even without grace. Man can perfect himself by his own efforts. Man does not need God's help in order to be united with God, to be perfectly happy in heaven. The result is seen today in a not-so-subtle form of semi-Pelagianism where man thinks he must do everything by his own power; he beats himself up over small mistakes; he prays so that God will empower him to do good on his own; he has "stress" because he cannot get everything done, especially morally good acts; he cannot forgive himself for his sins and continues in a feeling of guilt; and finally he turns toward lesser goods for fulfillment because he sees his futile efforts have not won him peace and happiness.

C. *Voluntarism*. Duns Scotus's idea of the nature of the will—voluntarism—was that the will is completely undetermined. Its nature is *to be undetermined*. It has nothing to do with goodness. This results in a theory of freedom where man must exert his will over his intellect and passions in order to be free from their influence. Every natural desire is to be eliminated so that the will can be completely free. The problem comes, however, with God's law which, being superior, must be obeyed. Only in such a case, according to Scotus, should man submit his will. The Christian life then becomes a matter of submission to God, and the highest virtue is obedience. This theory has the confusing and ironic effect of making man feel extremely unfree, and has generated a voluntaristic understanding of morality (for those who accept Christianity).

D. *Radical Autonomy.* William of Ockham took Duns Scotus's idea to its extreme, seeing the will as *radically indeterminate.* Ockham insisted that if man wills happiness necessarily, then he is not free.[27] Ockham believed that if the desire for happiness were part of man's nature, then it would be a necessity of force, and man would not then be free to choose against happiness.[28] For Ockham, man's will must become so "free" that it does not tend toward anything, not the good, not happiness, not anything. And then for it to be fulfilled, man's will must simply choose with nothing to hinder it, or inspire it, or influence it. This "freedom to choose" was Ockham's idea of complete fulfillment. Epitomized by the modern slogan "free choice," this is a perversion of Aquinas's idea of *liberum arbitrium.* According to Ockham's radical indetermination of the will, man's will

---

27. Simon Francis Gaine, *Will There be Free Will in Heaven? Freedom, Impeccability and Beatitude* (London: T&T Clark, 2003), pp. 71–73.

28. Ockham's confusion can be explained by the difference between the necessity of force and the necessity of nature. The necessity of nature is something natural in the sense that it follows from the necessity of the principles of nature, not in the sense of something that can be acquired by nature, like the natural virtues (see *De Veritate,* q. 24, a. 7, ad 10).

should be completely autonomous, subject to no one and no thing (not emotions, not intellect, not natural desire, and especially no other person).

Ockham's theory was that the nature of the will was to be completely arbitrary, not desiring anything (especially not the good) by its nature. The most important thing was for the will to be "free" from all influences of the senses, the emotions, and the intellect. Truth no longer has a bearing on the will. There is no such thing as a true good, and even if there was, the will must be completely free from having a tendency toward it. Freedom for Ockham meant complete "freedom" to choose.

For Ockham, only God could limit man's freedom. God's law was an exterior imposition, checking man's will, and is only obeyed out of slavish fear. God's will had no relation to truth, because man's will had no relation to truth. Goodness and truth did not really exist, so how could they govern action? What was left for Ockham? Only the will to choose. Modern conclusions include: "the deterioration of the idea of freedom into willfulness, the detachment of freedom from moral truth, an obsession with 'choice,' and the consequent inability to draw the most elementary moral conclusions about the imperative to resist evil."[29] Since Ockham believed that God's will was so completely sovereign, not related to anything like truth or goodness, that if God were to command man to hate Him, it would be good for man to hate God. The resulting moral theory is completely unstable, with the only moral precept being absolute autonomy of the will.

---

29. George Weigel, "A Better Concept of Freedom," *First Things* 121 (March 2002): pp. 14–20.

2. The denial of free choice.

A. *Lutheranism.* For Martin Luther, the will is not free, but is enslaved by sin. Therefore, man is not free. This presupposition had an effect on his entire theory of grace and on his view of Christianity as a whole. The consequences include, but are not limited to, the following: man does not have the ability to merit or demerit; receiving the sacraments is futile (especially confession); good works are futile; man is not responsible for his actions; man does not grow in grace or virtue (there is no such thing).

For Luther, grace can never overcome our degraded human nature. It only covers man's sins. Man is not sanctified from within. Grace cannot work in the very soul of man, nor purify him from inside. Man remains always corrupt in his soul.

If, as Luther thought, whatever man does, God does not do, and whatever God does, man does not do, then grace must not only be something exterior to man's will, but can never move man's will from within. According to Luther's view, salvation is solely on the part of grace, and man's will is not free in regard to his relation to God.[30] Karl Marx attributed this to the fact that there is only one level of being, "and what is granted to one must be taken away from the other. But where Luther chose God, Marx chose man."[31] The Reformers created an opposition between God and man in order to exalt God, to preserve His transcendence. It is only natural that someone would see it logical to do the opposite, to exalt man, as did Karl Marx.

---

30. Charles Morerod, *Ecumenism & Philosophy: Philosophical Questions for a Renewal of Dialogue*, trans. Therese C. Scarpelli (Ann Arbor, MI: Sapientia Press, 2006), p. 64.

31. Ibid., p. 113.

3. Denial of the existence of human nature (the philosophical roots of relativism).

A. *Jovinian (c. 340–409)*. Jovinian asserted that man cannot commit sin because everything given to his nature is good.[32] Related to Pelagianism, this idea promotes man as unable to sin. Starting with the truth that man's nature is good, Jovinian jumps to the conclusion that all of man's particular desires are therefore good, and then all of his acts are good. Therefore man cannot commit sin. Of course, with this idea grace is not needed. The idea is still seen today, usually with non-believers, in an "if it feels good, do it" mentality, but also with believers who see no need for confessing one's sins. Man might make intellectual mistakes, but not sins. In this view, man's will is confirmed in good, without grace. Jovinianism is sometimes hiding beneath the ability to accept responsibility for one's actions.

B. *Thomas Hobbes (1588–1679)*. Hobbes's theory was that there is no such thing as a common human nature, and therefore there can be no acts against nature. For Hobbes, morality is something invented by human beings because it is "mutually advantageous."[33] Men enter into "contractarian behavior" in order to gain their own advantages. Everyone has a right to do anything he wants, to choose any means to any end that he deems important. The best kind of man is the "rationally self-interested" man. Since we all benefit from not being killed, we all agree that murder is wrong. Morality, for Hobbes, is entirely a human invention, but men are better off adhering to it.

---

32. See *De Veritate*, q. 24, a. 12.

33. See Thomas Hobbes's "Moral and Political Philosophy," via the online Stanford Encyclopedia of Philosophy (2014).

C. *John Locke (1632–1704)*. Locke held that all universal concepts (such as good, truth, beauty, nature, etc.) exist only in the mind. Essences, and therefore natures (especially human nature), are completely made up by man, and are therefore not determined by anything outside of man. The problem this poses for morality is then that any universal "law" regarding moral action either comes from God, or cannot be determined by man based on anything objective. This is why, according to Locke, God must give commandments because God can be the only one to determine what is right and wrong. And even with this, God can change His mind. Again there are no moral absolutes (except that statement).

D. *David Hume (1711–1776)*. Hume thought that there is no such thing as the will. Man is simply a bundle of passions with an intellect for a slave. To say that something is "natural" to man meant that it is merely "statistically common" or "conducive to fitness."[34] All values are subjective to Hume (except for that statement). In agreement with Hobbes, Hume thought that morality is a human invention.

E. *Jean-Jacques Rousseau (1712–1778)*. For Rousseau, man is the same as an animal.[35] There is no such thing as

---

34. David Hume, *A Treatise of Human Nature: Being an Attempt to Introduce the Experimental Method of Reasoning into Moral Subjects* (London: John Noon, 1739). Hume writes, "Moral decisions are grounded in moral sentiment." He claims that reasoning has no relation to morality, but morality is based only on feelings (which is most probably included in the statement).

35. The addition of "rational" in the definition of man is only a pretext for Rousseau's idea of corrupt nature. Jean-Jacques Rouseau, *Discourse on the Origin and Foundation of Inequality Among Men*, [1755], trans. Donald A. Cress (Indianapolis, IN: Hackett Publishing Company, 1992), "Question," pp. 17–18: "The philosophers who have examined the foundations of society have all felt the necessity of returning to the

human nature. Rousseau believed that man's will is conditioned by circumstances and history so that a man is not truly free but only acts out of sensible desires, fears, or other passions. Morality is something extrinsic to man, not borne of man's true nature. There are no universal moral principles based on man's nature. Responsibility for one's actions, then, disappears and such a theory leads to educational and economic crises, where there is no right or wrong, no basis for understanding human nature, and only that which is

state of nature; but none of them has reached it… Religion commands us to believe that since God Himself drew men out of the state of nature, they are unequal because he wanted them to be so: but it does not forbid us to form conjectures, drawn solely from the nature of man and the beings that surround him, concerning what might the human race could have become, if it had been left to itself…"

And further, Rousseau says ("Part One," pp. 24–26): "In any animal I see nothing but an ingenious machine to which nature has given senses in order for it to renew its strength and to protect itself, to a certain point, from all that tends to destroy or disturb it. I am aware of precisely the same things in the human machine, with the difference that nature alone does everything in the operations of an animal, whereas man contributes, as a free agent, to his own operations. The former chooses or rejects by instinct, and the latter by an act of freedom. Hence an animal cannot deviate from the rule that is prescribed to it, even when it would be advantageous to do so, while man deviates from it, often to his own detriment… Every animal has ideas, since it has senses; up to a certain point it even combines its ideas, and in this regard man differs from an animal only in degree… Therefore it is not so much understanding which causes the specific distinction of man from all other animals as it is his being a free agent… Savage man, left by nature to instinct alone, or rather compensated for the instinct he is perhaps lacking by faculties capable of first replacing them and then of raising him to the level of instinct, will therefore begin with purely animal functions. Thus seeing and feeling must be his first condition, which would be common to him and all other animals. To will, and not to will, to desire and to fear, must be the first, and almost the only operations of his soul, till new circumstances occasion new developments of his faculties…"

convenient for the majority at any particular time governs all moral choices.

F. *Charles Darwin (1809–1882).* Darwin did not exactly deny human nature's existence, but insisted that at any moment man's nature may change. So for any practical purposes his conclusions about morality are the same. There can be nothing absolute about morality for man (except that statement).

4. Other aberrations of free choice.

A. *Manichaeanism (Albigensians).* The Manicheans asserted that man cannot in any way avoid sin because man is so inclined to follow the senses. Man should give up any effort toward virtue because there is no hope for him. Countered by St. Augustine in the late 400s and then again by St. Dominic in the 1200s, vestiges of this idea remain today, mixed with Lutheran and Jansenistic tendencies leading toward a depressing view of man as always choosing evil.

B. *Jansenism.* An offshoot of Albigensianism, Jansenism teaches that no one can receive grace unless he becomes worthy (somehow). Our sins make us so horrible in God's eyes, that God's anger is at the forefront of their spirituality. Vestiges of this idea are seen today when one believes that he is always ugly in God's sight, that God is punishing him and that is why he suffers, that he needs to prove himself in order to be worthy of God's grace, and eventually one need not pray or try to grow in virtue because he can never be worthy.

C. *Absolute moral relativism.* Seen in statements such as, "My truth is not your truth," and "That's true for you but not for me," and simply, "There is no truth," relativism has devastating effects on morality. Relativism is not simply the idea that three people might be seeing the same lake from three different points of view. Relativism is the firm conviction that the truth cannot be known (except for that statement), and that all things are relative (except for that statement), and that all truths can change (except for that statement), and there is no truth (except for that statement), and that if there are certain truths about God and about man, they are too difficult to know (except for that statement), and even if we do come to accept some concept of truth, truth is always changing (except for that statement). Therefore, one cannot be held to any responsibility regarding such knowledge, especially knowledge about moral questions (sigh of relief).

If human action has no relation to truth (either because truth cannot be known, or there is no truth, or simply we are not responsible for knowing it), then moral action must be based on something else. Otherwise, no one would ever act. The results are hedonism—pleasure is the only thing worth pursuing; co-existence—since there can be no truth on which to govern our actions (especially with regard to the state), we must have a government of "noninterference," or "toleration at all costs"; and, finally, tyranny—where might makes right, because there is no inherent right anyway.

Moral relativism is worse than the idea that "everyone should be able to do whatever they want as long as they don't hurt anyone." At worst, moral relativism allows for anyone to kill anyone else because there is no standard, no truth, no reason for judging moral action. Moral action then becomes a strange kind of balance between individualistic hedonism and external law. If there is a God (because this can never really be known either), God's law is (again) seen as an imposition, not as something that leads man to true fulfillment.

D. *Materialism.* Materialism says that only material things exist. There is nothing spiritual in this world. The resulting idea of freedom is that man can and should only desire (and therefore choose) goods that are material. Man cannot then really desire "freedom," because this cannot be embodied by some material good—except maybe enough money to make one feel comfortable, or free from physical suffering. Freedom from suffering is the main goal of materialists, with lesser goals of looking beautiful and having things. Materialism is seen in its banal form in those who simply have to "keep up with the Joneses." In its tyrannical form it is seen in those who cheat, steal, and kill in order to have more money, or power, or pleasure, or some other goal in this world.

E. *Utilitarianism.* For the utilitarian, that which is good is only that which is useful. The will might desire something not useful (like to gaze at a beautiful sunset), but this is not good. Therefore, one should only choose things that are useful to bring man to some desirable end (which also must be useful). Utilitarianism allows man to use another man as a means to an end. If the end is that all men be healthy, then utilitarianism says that it is fine to destroy all those who are not healthy. And it is fine to destroy other people so that one may be healthy. Since money is very useful, and sometimes necessary, many moral decisions for utilitarians are related to making money.

F. *Kantianism.* Reacting against utilitarianism, among other things, Kant invented a number of his own theories. For Kant, morality is grounded in reason; however, he did not think that reason could know reality. His distrust of reason, ironically, did not prevent him from asserting[36] that

---

36. Immanuel Kant, *Critique of Pure Reason*, trans. F. Max Muller (New York: Doubleday & Co., Inc., 1966). He says it in there somewhere.

reason has the ability to project categories on the world thereby making them objective. It is in this way that he "invented" his own moral principles, which on the surface resemble Christian principles. His "Categorical Imperative," for example, says something that we would agree with, that a human person is never to be used as a means to an end. However, for Kant, this imperative is not based on any objective idea of human nature (because there is no such thing, or if there is, it cannot be known), but it is based on the idea that the human mind has the ability to make laws and principles (not that laws and principles are discovered from observing nature).

One noticeable conclusion from this is of course that the human mind can choose to project some other "reality" at any moment. Coupled with his first categorical moral imperative—that one should only follow a principle if one can will it to become a universal law binding on all rational creatures—moral action is a matter of law that does not need to be based on something objective, but is completely subjective. Needless to say, the result is an emphasis on law which has no relation to truth or goodness. There would be very few moral laws, if any, unlikely to be aimed at a true good, and very little room for the Holy Spirit to inspire one's actions. Even Nietzsche called Kant a "catastrophic spider."[37]

G. *Nihilism (Nietzsche)*. Nietzsche took Ockham's idea of freedom to its logical conclusion. If God's will is the only thing left that can limit my will, then God must die. Nietzsche's famous idea of "will to power" is the ultimate

---

37. Friedrich Nietzsche, *The Antichrist*, quoted in *The Portable Nietzsche*, ed. and trans. Walter Kaufmann (New York: Viking, 1954), p. 11.

idea of a will that must be completely autonomous. All obstacles must be removed from my exercise of my own will. The result is the kind of nihilism that drives one to suicide, because very quickly man discovers that happiness does not result simply from doing whatever he wants. The results of his theory can be seen in Nietzsche's own actions, and in ideas like Peter Singer's insistence that parents ought to be able to wait a few weeks before they decide if their newborn child should be allowed to live.[38]

H. *The "Modern Misfit" position.* The position of the average modern person is that man wants to be good. There are good people who see that there must be objective moral norms, especially in the face of grave evils, but they do not know how to rationally defend the position. They have a strong intuition that every person has an inherent dignity. They see that history teaches us that strong cultural norms convince us that this is true. Otherwise, if man has no inherent dignity, then chaos results. And these observations convince modern man of the need for moral norms. The problem arises of course when faced with obstacles of clashing moral principles. History is not enough, conviction does not convince others, and cultures blend after time. If objective truth can never be known, morality cannot survive. Each person must act according to his conscience, and he cannot be judged on what he did not know.

VIII. The Truth about Freedom

The Catholic position regarding man's freedom is one that defends the truth of free choice and the reality of sin,

---

38. Weigel, *A Better Concept of Freedom.*

while maintaining the necessity of grace and the idea that freedom grows and develops.[39] The freedom of the sinner is preserved by avoiding these errors and making the proper distinctions.

Man does not lose his free choice as a consequence of sin. If this were the case, then man would be like an angel whose first act is complete.

So, if we accept Aquinas's exposé of the nature of the will, and therefore the nature of man's freedom, then may we conclude that all men will choose the good according to the nature of freedom? Unfortunately, this is not so easy. It is precisely Aquinas's account of the will that demands man's radical responsibility. In all of the above accounts, there are many ways for man to escape responsibility for what he wills. In Aquinas's view, man is responsible for everything that he wills, and accordingly he merits or demerits, and increases or decreases in his own freedom.

It is not the fact that the will has the possibility of choosing between contraries that gives the will the *ability* to choose.[40] It is the nature of the good that pulls on the will and is apprehended by the intellect that spurs man to seek and move toward the highest good, to choose according to that which appears more useful, more pleasant, or somehow best to him. It is not simply the ability to choose between contraries that gives the will its *impetus* to choose something. The power of the rational soul does not regard the nature of the contrary as such, but rather is open to contrary action because its faculties are not determined to one course

---

39. *De Veritate*, q. 24, a. 12.

40. See William of Ockham, *Opera Philosophica et Theologica*, ed. Gedeon Gál (New York: The Franciscan Institute, 1967–1988), pp. 319–21.

of action, or one good.[41] The will is open to many different aspects of good, and together with the intellect searches for the most useful good.[42] The act of fornication has an aspect of pleasure which is desired as a good, and making a vow of chastity has an aspect of good in binding oneself more closely to Christ, which is, in fact, a higher good of itself. A man may really struggle between choosing an act that is good or an act that is evil, but not because they are contraries. If his reasoning powers assesses the entire situation correctly, he will notice that he is attracted by certain goods, for certain reasons, and if he considers the circumstances correctly he will see that one attractive good lacks all of the necessary conditions for being a true good, and is therefore an evil act. This ought to make his concrete choice easier.

Man is not created for blind obedience or an unthinking execution of good acts. Man is called to a creative union of wills with the Trinity, where the harmony of responsible love results in fruitful activity, for the benefit of the individual soul as well as one's neighbor. In eternity, this love will continue, always active, surprisingly creative, and inexhaustible in comprehension. We will be truly "active" in heaven—eternally desiring and delighting in the true and supreme Good, God Himself.

---

41. *De Veritate*, q. 26, a. 3, ad 7.

42. *De Veritate*, q. 24, a. 6.

QUESTIONS

1. In what way(s) is the will both free and not free?

2. We are told that man is made in the image and likeness of God. Based upon this chapter, explain what this means. How does the reality of this relationship relate to freedom?

3. Is God's grace a threat to freedom? Why or why not?

4. When we pray the Our Father what are we asking for? How is conformity to God's will liberating? Give an example of a time when seeking God's will, and not your own, did not seem freeing. Why was this the case?

5. Summarize the major differences between the Freedom for Excellence and the Freedom of Indifference. Which view of freedom is most prevalent among your peers? Give an example.

6. How do the intellect and the will work together in the act of choice? What is each power seeking? What is the role of virtue in the act of choice?

7. Which theory of "wrong type of exultation of freedom" is most common today? Explain.

8. Which theory of "denial of free choice" is most common today? Explain.

9. Which "other aberrations of free choice" is most common today? Explain.

10. Use Section VIII, "The truth about Freedom," to create a rebuttal to the theories that you selected in questions #7–9.

APPLICATION

"For freedom Christ has set us free" (Galatians 5:1). When have you experienced a freedom to choose the good? What contributed to your ability to cooperate with God's grace? When have you experienced God's invitation as burdensome or rule-based? What contributed to your resistance?

APPENDICES

APPENDIX I:
FAITH AND THE EMOTIONS

Faith is a gift from God. It is the infused habit, perfecting the power of the intellect to know the truth and the will to love the good. Technically, faith does not *reside* in the emotions, but rather has an effect on them by elevating the faculties of intellect and will. When the intellect and will work together in the choice for a true good, the emotions share in the choice by desiring good in general (or averting from evil) before, during, and after the choice. The emotions themselves are not the faculties by which we choose, but they have a strong influence in daily decisions and are meant to be a support to man's search for, and final attainment of, ultimate happiness.

Faith is the avenue for the "rehabilitation" of the emotions, which are wounded (not made evil) by Original Sin. This is easily observed by experience. The stain of Original Sin, even after Baptism, renders the emotions with the tendency to become easily disordered. Faith, which is the beginning of the virtuous life, is necessary in order to provide the process for a remedy for the disordered emotions to become ordered again. To understand this mechanism of the soul, it is necessary to take a closer look at the nature of the emotions, both in general and in particular. To do this, we will follow the Master, St. Thomas Aquinas, by summarizing his treatise on the emotions in the *Summa Theologiae*.

The emotions are a component of the sensitive power of the human soul. The sensitive powers are those that we have in common with animals, which also have a sensitive nature, because we have a body with sense powers. Sight, hearing, smelling, tasting, and touch are the exterior sense powers. The interior sense powers are the common sense (which unites the exterior senses), the memory, the imagination, and the estimative sense. In addition, sensitive powers include the power of locomotion (self-movement) to a more or less sophisticated degree, and the eleven emotions.

Emotions are psychosomatic reactions to reality. The emotions are a gift of nature in the same way that eyes, legs, and arms are a gift of nature. Of themselves, they are morally neutral in their reaction to whatever is perceived. In fact, they are good in the sense that they help keep us alive. They initiate in us the desire to obtain good, or do good, and avoid evil or danger. The emotions automatically react to whatever one perceives to be good or evil, and will manifest that reaction through the body (increase in heart rate, red face, sweating, trembling, etc.). This is a sign that the man is alive and is in contact with reality. Notice also that the emotions react to what the intellect is perceiving as true. This is important. The emotions have a natural need to follow the intellect, to be guided by truth. For example, a man might become very angry if he finds that his car has disappeared from the parking lot, thinking that it was stolen. But if he finds out the truth, that really his wife traded cars with him and his car was not stolen, then his anger is diminished, if not completely assuaged, simply by knowing the truth of the situation.

So the emotions react to reality, and specifically, they react to whatever one thinks is good or evil. For any good perceived, there will be some (more or less proportionate) emotional reaction. And for any evil perceived, there will be a natural reaction of the emotions. This is for the good of the human being, mainly for the preservation of life and of the human species. Just as our nature is a gift from the Creator, so are our emotions a gift from the Creator—to be used for our individual and collective good. The fact that they are sometimes disordered tells us that some attention is required in order to re-align their operation.

The emotions are divided into two categories depending on the type of good or evil to which they are reacting. The concupiscible emotions react to a simple good or a simple evil; and the irascible emotions react to a difficult good or difficult evil. If one perceives a simple good and is attracted to it, whether or not that particular good is present here and now, the emotion that results is called love. So the emotion of love is a simple attraction to a simple good. If the simple good is not present, then the emotion is called desire. If the simple good is actually attained (present and united to the person), the emotion that results is called delight (or joy). This is the basic mechanism of the emotions; it implies that there is something good that is desired. When one perceives a simple evil, of any kind and in any way, the emotion that results is called hate. This is not willed hate, which is a sin, but simply the emotion of hate which does not want to be united with a perceived evil in any way. If the evil is not present to the person, the emotion that results is called aversion. When the evil is present, the emotion is called sadness. Sadness is our reaction to any perceived evil that cannot be avoided, or any lack of a good desired, especially a good that was present and is then taken away. Needless to say, guiding the emotion of sadness is very important for a faith-filled Christian life.

The second set of emotions react to good and evil, but with the added judgments of difficulty and possibility. The irascible emotions react to whatever the intellect perceives as a difficult good or a difficult evil. Notice that these emotions *require* an added judgment of the intellect, that something is difficult, making these emotions slightly more complicated. These emotions are therefore a little "closer" to the intellect and its judgment, and are sometimes more vehement, more strongly felt, because they result from a more intellectual conviction rather than a simple feeling of "I don't like it." If one judges a good to be difficult to obtain but not impossible, the resulting emotion is hope. This is not *willed* hope, the theological virtue of hope which is infused by God, but rather the *emotion* of hope, which is an emotional reaction to a difficult good. If one *judges* that the difficult good is *not* possible to attain, then one experiences the emotion of despair. Both hope and despair regard a good, not an evil. So it is not really possible to hope for an evil, or despair about an approaching evil. The most difficult good to attain is heaven, and that is usually the object of highest hope or deepest despair, although these emotions are felt with any difficult good which has not yet been attained. When the difficult good is attained the resulting emotion reverts again to the concupiscible emotion of delight, which you might remember is the emotion that results when any good is obtained.

In the case of the irascible emotions, however, there results a more intense delight because the good was that much more desired and required considerable effort to attain.

There are three emotions surrounding the perception of a difficult evil. If one perceives a difficult evil that is threatening, and one judges that it seems possible to overcome the evil, the resulting emotion is courage, or daring. This is not a "false bravado," a feeling of "I can do anything," but a feeling that relies on a judgment in the intellect of what one perceives to be really true. There is an evil threatening, but for some reason, one believes that one can overcome it—either by one's own ability, or the help of others, or the help of God. If one judges that it seems impossible to overcome the evil, that is not yet present but is coming, one experiences the emotion of fear. Both fear and courage regard an impending difficult evil, and differ according to the added judgment regarding the possibility or impossibility of overcoming it. Many times Jesus told His disciples, "Do not be afraid." Fear recognizes the reality of evil, and looks at human strength as the source for overcoming it. This happens so often, even to those with some degree of faith, that we need to be reminded often to "have faith in God," in order to overcome fear and allow the Holy Spirit to change our thinking and strengthen us. On the natural level, the deepest fear in man is fear of death, and this causes then the highest fear. Fear can paralyze man and keep him from acting according to the Holy Spirit. But "perfect love casts out fear." Love is actually the opposite of fear because love wants to be united to the true good at any cost, and will not be dissuaded by some difficult obstacle. (This is the reason why the "sappy love story" theme will never go out of style. It is built into our nature.) The true child of God looks to the strength of his heavenly Father, not self, for overcoming evil, and trusts in God's overpowering love to cast out all fear. It was out of love that Peter "put out into the deep," and Jesus was able to work miracles in him both before and after Peter's betrayal.

The emotion of anger, in Latin *ira*—from which the set of difficult emotions receives its name—is the last of the eleven emotions. Anger, which is the reaction to a difficult evil that is present and must be endured or fought, is the emotion which keeps the animal alive when its life is in immediate danger. Anger has the good effect of providing the human person with the energy necessary to act, such as extra energy to fight off an attacker, or to persevere through an ordeal, or to find creative ways of staying alive. Anger is a difficult emotion to control because it wants revenge in order to be assuaged, and will last as long as the perceived evil is present. When this goes on for a long time, it reverts to sadness, which causes more anger, and can turn into depression. Anger as an emotion is not a sin, as we can see from the example of Jesus in the Temple and the teaching of St. Peter, "Be angry but do not sin." Because of its vehemence and due to the reality of very difficult present evils, anger often leads one into a variety of sins (and is therefore considered dangerous, or even of itself causes fear), but of itself anger is a neutral emotion that can be used for good. It takes an adult about eighteen years (according to Conrad Baars) to learn how to deal with the emotion of anger. Like all the emotions, anger must be allowed to "run its course" as far as feeling it, and should not be "stuffed" behind a mask. Failing to admit the feeling runs the risk of causing further psychological harm. But rather, the emotions must be allowed to have their proper reactions, without necessitating a choice.

The emotions can become more complicated by reacting to other emotions, other people, other situations, in short, everything in reality. The phenomenon of repression occurs when the intellect judges a certain emotion to be "bad" and then reacts to that emotion, usually with fear or anger, in order to avoid the "bad" emotion. When the pattern becomes ingrained, the person does not understand that it is happening until the "bad" emotion explodes. The explosion, though not pleasant, is really necessary so that the pattern of repression can be stopped, and the person can deal with the "bad" emotion in a healthy way. "Anger issues" or sexual disorders are often indicators of a repressive tendency that developed, usually innocently, in childhood, out of some mis-information in the intellect. Somehow the child got the idea that sexual attractions were sinful (this will cause him or her to be afraid of natural desires and repress them), or somehow the child intuited that anger was unacceptable at home (and thus had to hide feelings of anger, rather than learn to express them appropriately and trustingly with parents). When repression is "uncovered," this is actually good news because the remedy involves a patient unfolding of the emotional traumas in the past, and healing does take place. With faith, the process is easier, maybe even faster, and part of the exciting principle that "the truth will set you free."

St. Thomas gives us a healthy respect for the emotions as gifts that can lead us to the Lord in every moment of life. For a healthy healing of the emotions, he gives us some advice: love the truth and seek the truth. This gives rational delight to the highest faculty of the soul, the intellect, and will have an effect on all the lower faculties by naturally ordering them. The lower faculties will have some rest when the highest faculty is at rest. Since the emotions have an effect on the body, St. Thomas tells us to give some reasonable pleasure for the body when negative emotions have to be endured (like sadness and anger). He suggests a hot bath, a strong drink (not too much), and we might add chocolate (which might not have been available to him in the Middle Ages) to give the body some comfort. For the comfort of the soul he recommends the enjoyment of friendship, or some kind of festivity or fun, even playing jokes, and the study of truth. For remedies of the emotion of anger in particular he adds the following: cultivate hope, practice forgiveness, remember death, exercise the virtues of humility and mercy, and most of all pray. The Lord knows us better than we know ourselves, and He wants to be with us in all of our experiences.

The emotions are meant to share in the free choice for a true good by the intellect and will, and are meant to help us to avoid a choice that really is evil or dangerous. "Unbridled" emotions lead to sin only because they entice the will and can blind the intellect. But "bridled" emotions can be trusted and have a proper interplay with the capacity for free choice. They are not meant to be ignored, but are deserving of an appropriate dignity. Aristotle's analogy of treating the emotions the way one treats a horse is well-taken. If a horse is gently but firmly guided by its master, the horse achieves its proper fulfillment, and makes a trustworthy and useful companion for man. But if the horse is whipped into submission, it rebels or sulks, and becomes useless to the master. So the emotions, sharing in man's true happiness, though not constituting it, must be guided by the intellect and will, and as such will help the virtuous man to love that which is truly good and to hate that which is truly evil for him. Faith, by opening man to knowledge of the true Good, as well as true evils, provides alignment for the will and for the emotions in moving toward that which is truly good. Thus the emotions themselves become avenues of grace for us, and have their proper share in the life of virtue. The emotions have their own proper dignity for man, providing man with energy and joy, to seek the true Good—that for which he was made—ultimately the perfection of love, union with God Himself.

Questions

1. How can faith contribute to the rehabilitation of the emotions? Give an example of a time when a more accurate understanding of a situation influenced and changed your emotional response.

2. Think of Jesus driving out the moneychangers from the temple. How can anger at injustice be channeled towards a zeal for making positive changes in the world?

3. Is there any idea or illustration from the appendix that particularly struck you? Why?

APPLICATION

C. S. Lewis, in *The Great Divorce*, illustrates the rehabilitation of the emotions in terms of a whispering, controlling lizard on a man's shoulder being transformed through a mysterious death into a mighty steed that the man can ride to the hills' heights. Paradoxically, it is the surrender of our emotions to reason and grace that gives the emotions their full flourishing and power. Why do we often forget the glorious truth that the emotions are part of man's perfection in this life and even in Heaven? What are practical ways that we can remind ourselves of this truth?

APPENDIX II:
A NOTE ON REPRESSION

According to Conrad Baars, the experience of the repressed person is that these repressing emotions

> begin to operate for the purpose of getting rid of those emotions and feelings which he thinks are bad, sinful, unacceptable to others, or cause hurt in himself or other people. The child may be informed correctly about everything else in the world, go to the best schools and so on, yet if he is given incorrect information, directly or indirectly, about the nature and function of his emotions, he has no choice but to react to this misinformation by repression, i.e., by pushing those emotions into his subconscious when he feels them. The same happens when he is given the right information, but prematurely, when he is too young to understand it.[1]

As the repression continues, it causes him to have a more and more difficult time *choosing* to resist the emotion's object, and instead relies on the action of a stronger emotion to repress the unwanted emotion.

The unhealthy reaction in repression is not due to the fact that one emotion causes another emotion, such as a person who gets angry at himself whenever he feels fearful, or one who feels fear whenever he feels anger welling up. Nor is it due to the fact that the emotions react to one's own judgments. Particular judgments regarding the usefulness or harmfulness of objects are linked to the estimative sense but not completely reliant on it because information is also gathered from the intellect,[2] and an emotional reaction to one's own judgment is good and useful. To have emotional factors influence rational choices is not of itself bad, and in fact is meant to aid us, as explained earlier. The unhealthy reaction is the uncontrolled action of repressing emotions which completely escape the cooperation of the intellect and will.

A common type of repression involving fear is seen when fear is used as a control for behavior. For example, a child might be deterred from stealing a cookie due to fear of punishment. It is hoped that if the child does not see the rationality of the rule, at least the fear of punishment will keep him from doing the act. In an emotionally healthy child, eventually the fear will become subordinated to the

---

1. Baars, *Feeling and Healing*, pp. 129–30.

2. Baars, *Psychic Wholeness and Healing*, p. 35: "Because of the influence of the intellect, this power (the estimative power) is able to form a particular judgment regarding the usefulness and harmfulness of objects, and this judgment is not determined solely by the ability to attain a certain concrete sense good."

intellect's judgment that it is wrong to steal, or it is not good to disobey, or that it will ruin his appetite for dinner. As he grows older he will be able to make a more rational choice to refrain from stealing the cookie, and the fear will hopefully disappear. We might also say that the healthy child will not let his fear overtake him, and might sometimes steal the cookie, judging that the cookie is worth the suffering of the punishment (if it were a double-stuffed Oreo cookie, for example, this would be perfectly reasonable). This child who seems to be disobedient might actually have a better chance at developing a healthier emotional life, and thus be able to develop the integration necessary for true obedience later on in life.[3] The unhealthy reaction might appear to be virtuous on the exterior, where the child strictly obeys the rules, but never fully develops in his emotional life because he has always obeyed only out of fear of punishment. This kind of emotional immaturity usually ends in either rebellion or depression of some kind.

When fear-based repression is traced back to an erroneous interpretation of reality, it is especially damaging. At some point there was a conscious rejection of something which is truly good as something harmful to be feared and avoided.[4] An example of this kind of repression is seen where the desire for sexual pleasure is seen as harmful, which is

---

3.   See Conrad Baars, "Psychological Aspects of Obedience," in *I Will Give Them a New Heart: Reflections on the Priesthood and the Renewal of the Church*, ed. Suzanne Baars and Bonnie Shayne (New York: Society of St. Paul, 2008), pp. 105–144.

4.   Baars, *Psychic Wholeness and Healing*, p. 52: "Except for very young children, the initial repression must have been the result of a conscious recognition of something—which is actually good—as harmful and its conscious repudiation."

not in accord with natural instinct. It would have to have been "learned" somehow, that this natural desire or pleasure is not good. This happens if the intellect believes that the sexual desire is harmful or sinful of itself (perhaps having been taught Jansenistic propaganda), or if a concomitant emotion, such as fear, was aroused at the same time and blocked the emotion for pleasure. This can happen if a child learns about sexual information too early or is taught *in such a way* that fear is also aroused in him. To a certain extent, it is natural and normal for the irascible appetite to have a reaction when the sexual desire is activated (usually in service of the concupiscible appetite), and this is why teenagers are expected to be slightly confused. But the problem comes when the irascible emotion, usually fear, either blocks or inhibits, consciously or unconsciously, the guidance of the concupiscible emotion by the free choice. When this happens, emotions of the pleasure appetite are no longer guided by reason and will, but will be guided, partially at least, by the irascible appetite, causing confusion and possibly aberrant behavior.[5]

Another type of repression can occur due to an emotional reaction to the intellect's judgment. For example, if the intellect excessively makes judgments regarding the usefulness of a thing, and the only value given to something will be its usefulness, then the pleasure appetites can become starved or squashed. The concupiscible appetite will eventually bubble to the surface and cause trouble—over-eating or under-eating, drinking, other addictions, etc.—because man cannot live without some kind of pleasure. The intellect has accepted the false belief that usefulness is a higher

5. Ibid., p. 36.

good to such an extent that it excludes pleasure itself. The role of the intellect in repression is subtle but necessary in adults for the process to begin. Knowledge is either received with accompanying emotions, or causes an emotional reaction, and this conditions the thought process, or bypasses it altogether, and therefore ensnares the free choice. Baars explains:

> It is not what a person *knows*, or *believes* to be true, about emotions, human drives and human nature that leads him to repress, but rather his emotional reaction to these beliefs. His *fear* or *emotional energy* constitute the repressive force which moves him to try to get rid of feelings and ideas which he is led to believe are socially unacceptable, if not morally wrong. His emotional reaction does not depend so much on the actual teachings themselves, as on the emotional atmosphere in which they are presented.[6]

Here we might be tempted to say that it does not matter if the intellect holds as true something that is false, because the emotional reaction is what causes the repression. While that is true, we can see that repression is more likely to happen if the intellect believes something that is false, for example that attraction to the opposite sex is not good, and then this belief causes an emotional quandary, because the intellect will not be able to stop the sense appetites from being attracted to a good in accord with nature. More importantly, however, is the emotional atmosphere that is felt by the one receiving the formative knowledge. The emotional reaction

---

6. Baars, *Feeling and Healing*, pp. 132–33.

will supersede the intellectual information, especially in young children, when it comes to moral formation. If a child senses emotionally that something is bad, even though he repeats the words that it is good, his emotions will not accept it. This is because all information is received first through the senses. The emotions are valid and automatic reactions, and cannot be ignored. As the human being moves from the predominance of the emotional life to the predominance if the intellectual life, it seems that the transition needs to be smooth and take place over time. For this reason, the emotional life develops within the safety of the family, and requires a transition when new scenarios are experienced.

If a repressed emotion is left buried alive, it can expand in different ways. Usually unconsciously, the repression can spread to include similar objects (first the sexual desire is repressed, then sex itself, then the sense of touch, then the sense of taste, and finally all feelings). The repression can also resurface under different urges, such as uncontrollable eating habits, abnormally collecting things, a pathological need for recognition and appreciation, workaholism, or an intense desire for religious experience.[7]

The cure is not simply to express and bring to fulfillment all emotions. The cure is to accept and allow oneself to *feel* all one's emotions, knowing that they are not equal to the movement of the will. Just as if a knife cuts one's finger and blood is expected to pour out, if a certain cupcake is brought into the room, a certain emotional reaction can be expected. All emotions must be felt, but not necessarily expressed.[8] That is, they are allowed to be what they are,

---

7.   Baars, *Psychic Wholeness and Healing*, pp. 53–56.

8.   Baars, *Feeling and Healing*, p. 109.

responses to reality, while the intellect and will remain free to gently integrate and guide them. All good things should bring us pleasure, especially the higher goods:

> What ultimately matters is what man strives for, not the striving itself. When, from all the possible objects which can stimulate his pleasure appetite, man chooses that which is most proper to him as man, it will be only through the subordination of the utility appetite to the pleasure appetite that he can do full justice to his human nature.[9]

The estimative sense together with the irascible emotions plays a role eventually in all man's acts, except those which are purely pleasurable. Hence we see that the main focus of the emotions is really geared toward the enjoyment of true goods,[10] and a repression of the pleasure appetite itself will be the most damaging of all because a man will not be able to take pleasure in his highest good.

---

9. Baars, *Psychic Wholeness and Healing*, p. 16.

10. Ibid., pp. 15–16: "Because of the subordination of the utility appetite to the pleasure appetite, the *main accent in the emotional life must naturally rest on the pleasure appetite*, and not on the utility appetite. When the emphasis is shifted to the utility appetite, there is a disharmony of the emotional life, with potentially disastrous consequences to the psychic life."

QUESTIONS

1. Why does repression make free choice difficult?

2. How is fear-based repression often linked to an incorrect judgment on the part of the intellect? Why, then, is it so crucial to "reform" our judgments?

3. What qualities should characterize the role of the intellect and will in relating to the emotions as we strive for integration?

4. How might good counsel and friendship help towards emotional integration and freedom?

APPLICATION

What foundational principles from this book will you carry with you into your study and living out of Christian morality?

CLUNY MEDIA

Designed by Fiona Cecile Clarke, the CLUNY MEDIA *logo depicts a monk at work in the scriptorium, with a cat sitting at his feet.*

The monk represents our mission to emulate the invaluable contributions of the monks of Cluny in preserving the libraries of the West, our strivings to know and love the truth.

The cat at the monk's feet is Pangur Bán, from the eponymous Irish poem of the 9th century. The anonymous poet compares his scholarly pursuit of truth with the cat's happy hunting of mice. The depiction of Pangur Bán is an homage to the work of the monks of Irish monasteries and a sign of the joy we at Cluny take in our trade.

"Messe ocus Pangur Bán,
cechtar nathar fria saindan:
bíth a menmasam fri seilgg,
mu memna céin im saincheirdd."

Made in the USA
Middletown, DE
23 December 2021

55629783R00070